INVESTING 201

Safer, Simpler and More Effective

MATTHEW S. BARNES

© Matthew S. Barnes, 2019

All rights reserved. This book or any portion thereof may not be reproduced or used in any manner whatsoever without the express written permission of the publisher except for the use of brief quotations in a book review. Printed in the United States of America.

First Printing, 2019

https://www.amazon.com/-/e/B00SDYKSZ2

https://www.matthewbarnes-101.com/

DISCLAIMER

The information contained in this book is for general information purposes only. Any reliance you place on such information as listed in this book is strictly at your own risk. The author or publisher of this book will not be held liable for any loss or damage including without limitation indirect or consequential loss or damage, or any loss or damage whatsoever arising from loss of data or profits arising out of or in connection with the use of information in this book or the websites it mentions. We have no control over the nature, content and availability of other sites. The inclusion of any links does not necessarily imply recommendation or endorse the views expressed within them. Every effort is made to keep our website up and running smoothly. However, we take no responsibility for, and will not be reliable for, the website being temporarily unavailable due to technical issues beyond our control. There is inherent risk in investing. Past performance does not guarantee future results.

ACKNOWLEDGMENTS

I'd like to thank all of my supporters, as usual, as well as to acknowledge Robert Kiyosaki, Ken Roberts, Ted Warren, Warren Buffett, Burton H. Pugh, Dave Ramsey and all the other non-conventional money thinkers and traders out there who had the fortitude to buck the accepted way of doing everything and make a new path. I understand the rarity of such a thing, and truly appreciate what you have been able to do.

I'd like to thank Ken Roberts again, this time for pointing out that investing is as much emotional as it is mental. Mr. Roberts consistently recommended reading books on developing a calm, mental fortitude and not only on the technical aspects of training. I'd like to suggest the same to you. You seriously need the calm of a zen master when the markets start to buck and roll.

I'd also like to acknowledge all the warriors out there that are actually investing and not just talking about it. After my first investing book was published, I found out very quickly that there are hordes of people out there with no actual experience in investing who have absolute, unwavering opinions on the subject. How curious.

CONTENTS

INTRODUCTION 9
THE OUTLINE...........................13
I'M NO EXPERT.........................15
THE EXPERTS AREN'T EXPERTS EITHER 17
THIS IS NOT DAY TRADING 19
IF THIS STUFF WORKS,
    WHY DO I NEED TO WRITE BOOKS?..............22
NOBODY CARES FOR YOUR
    MONEY AS MUCH AS YOU DO...................24
INDIAN RETIREMENT INVESTING 26
HOW MUCH DO YOU NEED TO RETIRE ON? 28
SETTING UP YOUR RETIREMENT FUND............31
PENSIONS................................33
YOUR RETIREMENT BILL 34
BUFFETT WINS A BET!............................35
THE CONSERVATIVE RETIREMENT FUND..........37
ACCELERATING RETIREMENT,
    ACCELERATING WEALTH 40
FINDING MORE MONEY TO INVEST................42
PAYING OFF DEBTS and CREATING A SAFETY NET ..47
THE AGGRESSIVE, EARLY RETIREMENT FUND 50
THE AGGRESSIVE, EARLY RETIREMENT FUND LIST 55
THE AGGRESSIVE,
    EARLY RETIREMENT FUND LIST, part 2...........56

MY LEVERAGED ETF LIST 61
THE FASTEST RISING............................64
INVESTING IS EMOTIONAL 68
WHEN TO EXIT AN INVESTMENT 72
NEARING RETIREMENT AND
    MY NEWEST EXPERIMENT......................76
CLARIFYING MY STRATEGY 84
FUNDAMENTALS VS TECHNICAL ANALYSIS........86
PAPER TRADE FIRST............................89
AFTER THE MORTGAGE AND/OR
    STUDENT LOANS ARE PAID OFF 93
I AM STILL LEARNING............................95
RIDING THE CYCLES 97
DON'T LISTEN TO THE NEWS,
    OR OTHER PEOPLE............................100
WHAT ABOUT OPTIONS? 103
WHAT ABOUT IRAs,
    401Ks AND THINGS LIKE THAT? 104
PROTECTING YOUR GOLDEN EGG! 107
KEEPING UP WITH YOUR PROGRESS 110
A DREAM COME TRUE- LIVING OFF
    YOUR INVESTMENTS 113
SIMPLIFIED SUMMARY AND ACTION STEPS.......117
YOU VS YOU, BEFORE AND AFTER.................119
SHAMELESSLY PUSHING
    MY NEWSLETTER SERVICE 120
FURTHER RESOURCES..........................122
BIO 125
LETTER FROM THE AUTHOR....................127

INTRODUCTION

As I explained in my first investing book, *Investing 101*, I want to be free of the tyranny of money. I want to be free to do whatever I want to do, and still have enough money to survive. I do want to contribute to society, but I also hate being at the whim of money. Spiritual issues aside, money controls us, one and all. And I don't like it one bit.

I believe that money is freedom- at least with how our world works currently. I hope that this book will help us both to reach that freedom. Freedom from the tyranny of money, freedom to do what we want to do, and freedom to be what we want to be, without having to worry so much about money.

This book will be short, direct, and straight to the point. I don't really believe in fluffing up my method of investing in order to make it sound better, more complicated or more credible. What I have been doing works, and I'm going to show you how to do it in as few words as possible. You may be able to read my entire book and absorb my entire method in a single reading, in a single day. My method of investing is a very, very simple and boring method.

This book will have a lot of the same information and the same outline as my first book on the subject. In fact, I wrote this version on the "skeleton" of the original work, so a lot of it will sound the same. The main difference between my first investing book and this updated version will be when you get to the investing method- both in choosing investments and in knowing when to get in and when to get out of them. My new method is quite different. Over the years I have learned, gained experience and gotten better at investing. This book will update what I do now compared to what I used to do. What I do now makes me much more money than the old way, and with less risk. I sleep much better at night. Please note though, that you need to read through to the end, for I give you both my current method of investing, as well as, later on in the book, my newest strategy that I am experiementing with.

I will also be brutally honest with you. I will not exaggerate or try to fool you. Most investing methods out there point out instances where unbelievable returns have happened with their methods. What they do not tell you is that this type of thing does not happen often, and when it does, the person that made such a crazy return on their investment typically goes on to lose those gains and more down the road, showing just how volatile their approach can be.

I will also be pushing my weekly newsletter quite a bit in this book. Since my first book, I have found, in no uncertain terms, that investing correctly is highly emotion and completely counterintuitive. If you really want to make money, you will have to do exactly opposite of what your instincts may be telling you to do, and opposite of what everybody else is doing. This can be very hard to do.

Most people buy into an investment once excitement is high and the investment is rising quickly. This is usually too late to get in, because these fast rises do not last that long, and that investment is most likely close to a drawback or correction.

INTRODUCTION

When the drawback or correction hits, the average person gets scared and exits the investment, usually at a loss. They are buying high and selling low, when the opposite is what is needed to make money. But it is so counterintuitive to do the opposite of what everyone else is doing that most people simply cannot do it. Thus the newsletter.

The above image outlines how most people invest.

I have found, over and over and over again, that regular people that want to invest need their hands held. This is not an insult. We are all seeing on television and hearing from friends and even family members what everyone else is doing with their money. We are herd animals, and need to feel that we are part of the herd, doing things similarly to everyone else. We think that the herd must be correct. We feel that if we are doing something different from the herd, then we are wrong and are going to pay for it. It scares us.

I have a close friend who is also a member of the newsletter that is now making very good money investing. She gets so excited. She is absolutely on the path to an early and very profitable retirement. However, every single time the market has a big correction, or even a medium one, we have to have long, drawn out, reassuring talks about how everything is ok. She has to be reassured regularly until the markets turn, then she is ecstatic again.

My newsletter is my way of holding your hand, showing you exactly what I am doing, when I am doing it, just like I do with her.

Seriously, investing is hard. It is very emotional. Most of us need help, need reassurance, at least in the beginning, until we get used to the tides of the markets.

Plus, to be brutally honest, having a newsletter is another avenue of income for me. I charge a mere $10 a month for my newsletter. It is absolutely worth it for you, no doubt in my mind, and a stream of income for me. If you don't make that $10 a month back in the information you get, then something has gone very wrong.

For more information on the newsletter, go to: https://www.matthewbarnes-101.com/the-money-club-newsletter.

THE OUTLINE

Let's jump right in and give you the basic outline, the basic gameplan, of my system- it consists of two investment funds:

1. The first thing we are going to do is to figure out how much money you want to retire on comfortably, at a bare bones minimum, and at what age you want to try and retire.

    Using a free online calculator, we will estimate how much we need to put away every month in order to hit that retirement goal.

    We will pay that amount each and every week or month into our investment portfolio like it is a bill. That money will be invested conservatively. We are trying to assure, at the very least, a comfortable and timely retirement.

2. Next, we will use a little money management to find money that you will use to pay off your debt.

3. Once your debt is paid off, the money you had been using to pay off your debt will be added to a second investment fund. This fund's aim is to accelerate your retirement, and will be invested much more aggressively.

The overall goal of this system is to create and live off your very own money tree. You put money in, grow that money, and eventually live off of that money. In the end, you will hopefully leave that money tree to your kids when you are gone.

People that grew up without money tend to look at money differently than people who have had money their entire lives. People not used to money tend to spend money as they make it. They buy things like cars and houses. They even spend more than they make by buying on credit.

The rich do it differently. They take the money they earn and instead of spending it once, they find a way to live off of it forever. They buy things like rent houses, other real estate, and invest it in the market. In this way, they live off the returns on their money but never touch the actual principle. They make money once and live off of it forever.

Those not used to money do the exact opposite. They spend what they make, and then some, usually.

I will also show you how to protect your money from predators.

Let's get started.

I'M NO EXPERT

The first thing I want to make clear in this little book is that I am no expert. I have no financial degrees; I have no license to be a broker or financial advisor or anything even close to any of that. I am simply a man that got fed up with having other people manage his money.

If you are the type of person that is only interested in information coming from someone with a long list of degrees after their name, I'm definitely not the person for you. If you are the type of person that is easily swayed by the opinions of others, or the "experts" on TV, then this system is not for you. What I do and what the "experts" on TV and the financial advisors will tell you to do are usually very different. I have tried to help several friends make money that got in an investment too late and got out too late because they were too scared not to listen to the experts on TV. As a result, many of the people I have tried to help invest in the past have lost money on the very same investments that I made money with.

If you are still with me, and you are one of these independent people that can and do swim against the tide of the masses if you think that you are right and that they are wrong, then there is a different problem we need to talk about with you. It is best for you to "paper trade" for a while until you are sure you have the hang of this system. Paper trading is when you pretend to trade and keep up with your results, but you aren't using real money yet. Often, independent people get a little too independent and jump right in head-first. Even though you may catch on quickly, there is something about experience that can't be rushed. So in the beginning, go slow- paper trade, and when you do start using real money, only invest in small amounts initially. You don't want to jump in head-first with all the money you have and then find out you didn't quite understand a thing or two.

THE EXPERTS AREN'T EXPERTS EITHER

One of the reasons I ended up doing my own investing is that I found out that the people we rely on to handle our money aren't actually experts at handling our money. I am not trying to put down any brokers or financial advisors, for we all have to make a living, but what I discovered is that these guys are really just salesmen.

What happens is that brokers and financial advisors are trained in the rules of their trade and the laws and guidelines of investing, and then they are trained on how to get clients. These guys are very rarely trained in or know much about investing at all. Their job is to get you as a client, then the higher ups in the company tell them which investments to sell you.

Your broker or advisor gets a percent of the money you invest with them. They don't want you to ever take that money out, no matter what is going on in the market, because if you do, they lose money, and so does their company. The idea that you should always stay in the market "no matter what" came from these large companies. It is not necessarily for your benefit that they say this. It is for the benefit of the company and for the benefit of your advisor. Big companies have pushed this idea for so long that it has become a common thought in the world of investing, and is taken as "the gospel truth" by many people.

Remember that even those we are taught to see as "experts" at growing your money usually are not. What they *are* good at is getting clients, selling investments to those clients and keeping those clients from ever leaving those investments.

The criticisms I have gotten in my investing method so far are mostly from financial investors that do not like what I say. I do not blame them. Not all of them are bad. They have to make a living too. But they tend to not argue with me about results. They argue because my way of doing things, in theory, goes against what they were taught and is therefore considered bad. The problem is that they are all arguing theories and academic definititions. I am not about to argue with them about those things. My argument is based on one thing and one thing only- results. I don't care how many big words you can use, how many years you spent in school, or how many clients you have- my only question is how good are your results?

THIS IS NOT DAY TRADING

Some of you may be looking for a "get-rich-quick" type of system. This is not what my method is about. My method is not day trading, or any other type of system that requires constant attention. Nor is it a "bag of tricks". My method of investing is an overall system, an understandable strategy, an actual understanding of how to best handle your money and how to best take advantage of the way the market tends to run. You will not learn incomprehensibe terms and tricks, but will hopefully come to understand how the markets tend to run and how to intelligently position yourself in a way that will best capitalize on this knowledge. My system is very simple.

The ultimate goal is to live off your money instead of *having* to work for your money. I am going to show you how to put the money you are working for to work for you. I am going to show you how to turn the money you are earning into more and more money until you can eventually get out of the "rat race" and live off of your investments. When you get to this point, you can still work if you *want* to, but you don't *have* to. If you do still decide to work, you can do what you *want* to do, not what you *have* to do.

But you do have to be patient. Think in terms of years and maybe even decades, not days or weeks or months. Day traders want it now. Typical investors, on the other hand, are thinking very long term. I am talking somewhere in between. Do not expect immediate results, but do aim to do better and quicker than the long term investors. What we are doing is stalking our retirement. We are intelligently setting up a medium to longer-term plan that, if we stick with it, will eventually support us.

Most people make money and then they spend it all. This is the normal average. They work hard for their money, but then only get to spend that money *once*. You are going to learn how to "earn" the money once, but spend it *forever*. You are going to start taking some of the money you physically earn, invest it, turn it into more money, and eventually make enough off of your "money generator" that you can live off your money instead of having to earn every dime forever. You are going to start putting some of that money into investments to make that money *work for you* instead of *you working for it*. Eventually, when you have enough money invested, you will be able to live off the interest you earn from that investment. Say you save up a million dollars, and say you make 10% per year on your money, which is about average, your money is now earning you $100,000 per year without you doing much of anything. You never touch the base of one million dollars; you only spend some of the interest that spins off of it. You now have a money tree. You pick its leaves, but leave the rest of the tree alone.

But you will have to be patient. A lot of people have read this book, gotten really excited, joined the newsletter and then quit after three to six months because they weren't rich yet. Unless you are already beginning with quite a bit of money, you are not going to become wealthy overnight. And even if you do already have quite a bit of money, depending on the phase of the market, it still may take time for the money tree to develop. This is not all going to take place in three to six months, which seems to be how long the average person is willing to give it. I think most people that quit early were expecting constant excitement, a constant rise in money. Investing just doesn't work that way. Instead, it is going to take years to grow your money. And there are going to be entire years of downturn, where you make little to no money, or even lose a little. You must be patient. Try for too much too fast and you will most likely sink your boat. You may hit a home run here or there, but you will strike out way too often to accumulate any real wealth. At least that has been my experience in the past, both with myself and with my observation of others.

Proper investing is long and boring and tedious, with lots of ups and downs, twists and turns. I can't emphasize this enough. Improper expectations will lead only to dissatisfaction. If you do decide to invest, or if you do decide to get my newsletter, expect, for the most part, for investing to be boring. Even when we have good runs, they take place over months, not a single day. And if the market does jump quite a bit one day, it'll take most of it back the next. My strategy is a medium to longer term strategy that plays on the best probabilities over the medium to longer term. The market tends to average at least 3 years of uptrend to one year of down. In the last 28 years, that comes to 21 good years and 7 bad. This is a good average, in our favor. It indicates an upward overall tendency. Invest correctly, postion yourself intelligently, and you take advantage of this tendency. If, in addition, you then invest in the fastest rising investments, you will accelerate the growth of your money quite a bit.

Remember, at all times, that investing is about probability. You are simply trying to best position yourself to take advantage of what is most probable, and then leverage the outcome to the greatest possible extent. There are no guarantees, only high probabilities and low probabilities.

IF THIS STUFF WORKS, WHY DO I NEED TO WRITE BOOKS?

This is a very, very good question, and you should always ask this question of anyone claiming to have any kind of secret money making knowledge. Here is my answer:

I'm not where I want to be yet. It's as simple as that. I do feel like I have a good, solid, safe system. I do feel like it is *much* safer than letting someone else handle my money. I do feel like I make great returns, and have grown a small amount of money into a much larger pile. BUT, it takes money to make more money. I started trying to figure this system out maybe fifteen or twenty years ago. I got bruised and roughed up as I went. I lost a lot of money along the way. I learned as I went. I kept studying. I kept trying, and now I feel confident that my system is at least as good as any body else's out there that I have come across, but much easier and simpler to actually do. And more honest. Most years I beat the S&P. You won't need a PhD or a business degree to follow, though you will need some will power, some determination and some general "stick-with-it-ness" in order to get by the early stages of growing your money.

The beginning is the hardest. You don't have much, and the less you have the slower the growth you will see, and that's just not exciting. But once it starts to grow, it gets fun. There are still times along the way when you will get frustrated, irritated, angry, scared and you

IF THIS STUFF WORKS, WHY DO I NEED TO WRITE BOOKS?

will wish the market would just climb up gradually and consistently and stop stalling, falling, jumping around, and all the other things it tends to do. If you stick with it, when the smoke clears, the long-term picture is great. If you get impatient and impulsive or scared you can really mess up the long-term picture.

So again, why listen to me? If I were that good with stocks I wouldn't have to publish a book! The answer is that I just am not retired yet. I am still plagued by the tyranny of money, but I am climbing out of that pit. I got a late start in investing, it took me years to start doing well, and now I am making up for lost time. But money makes money. I need more money from writing and doing my newsletter so that I have more money to invest in order to reach my own goal of retiring early, living off my investments, and doing the work I *want* to do. I also have run into several issues, including divorce, where my assetts keep getting split in half. This is a major, major drawback that I hope most of you can avoid.

I know most investors writing books claim to have taken a single dollar and turned it into a billion. I have tried out many of their systems and have not found it to be true. Like I said before, I am going to be brutally honest with you. I make great returns, but realistic returns. I'm not promising you a fairy tale investment plan.

I am also wrting this book and doing the newsletter because I very much enjoy learning and helping others with what I have learned.

NOBODY CARES FOR YOUR MONEY AS MUCH AS YOU DO

Ken Roberts, a famous self-investment guru, used to say this a lot. And it is completely true. Nobody cares about your money as much as you do. NOBODY! I figured this out the hard way. And I have watched several friends also figure this out the hard way. Look at all the financial scandals that have been in the news the last few years- AIG, Bernie Madoff, and the housing crisis to give just a few examples. Your best interests are not anywhere on the priority lists of these guys at all, much less at the top of their priorities. But examples of why you need to manage your own money don't even have to be on such a grandiose scale.

I have three friends that would have retired very comfortably had it not been for the stock market plummet right after the terrorist attacks of 9/11, and if their financial advisors would have taken them out of the market as directed. One lady, as an example, who had recently lost her husband, had about a million dollars saved and invested. When the market started going down she asked her financial advisor to take her out of the market for a while, maybe put her into something like a money market or bonds or something. The advisor spoke down to her and basically refused to take her money out as she requested. When the smoke cleared her nest egg of a million dollars had dropped to somewhere around $250,000. And right at her retirement age. Now, instead of enjoying her retirement as she had earned the right to do, she is really having to watch her money, and even ended up having to take a part time job to get by. She is in her upper 70s and still has to work.

I have other very similar stories that I won't bore you with, but the point of the story is that NOBODY CARES ABOUT YOUR MONEY AS MUCH AS YOU DO!! The bottom line for me is that if you want someone who *truly* cares about your financial future to control your money, then that person needs to be you. There are two advantages to being in control of your money. First, you do not have to pay anybody else fees to manage your money, therefore you get to keep more of it. Secondly, YOU control when and if you need to take your money out and sit on the sidelines a bit in order to protect your nest egg.

I believe you can make the same (if not better) returns on your money as the "experts" with this simple system, and much more safely, because *you* are in charge.

INDIAN RETIREMENT INVESTING

I met a young lady from India at a seminar a few yeasrs back and we started talking about investing. As I was telling her about the system I use, and about my theory of spending your money forever instead of spending it only once she got really excited. Evidently, this idea is a given among the people of India. They work hard and save as much money as they can when they are young. When they get enough money saved, they buy a business (like a dry cleaning business) and hire people to run it for them, often younger family members. Then they retire and live off the income from the business, which they don't even have to physically work in. They have turned money that they earned into a money generator. This is how they save for retirement.

I look at investing the same way- as a business. You work hard, save your money and then you invest that money. When you invest, you are actually buying shares of companies. As these companies make profits, you share in the profits. Profits you don't have to work for. The companies you have shares in are doing the work. This is passive income. Income you are not physically working for. You are taking your hard earned money and putting it into a money generator, just like Indian retirees do.

I like my way better though. What I like better about my business is that I don't have to hire any employees as the Indians do when they buy a physical business. The more employees you have the more headaches you have. Ask any business owner. You may love your employees to death, but they still complicate things. You have to find them, you have to train them, and you have to find replacements when they are sick or when they quit.

But the overall idea is the same, whether you retire like the Indians by buying a physical business, or, like I do, by buying shares of companies. Either way, you work hard, save your money and buy a money generator with your hard earned cash instead of spending it all.

HOW MUCH DO YOU NEED TO RETIRE ON?

My favorite method of figuring out how much money you need to be putting away in order to retire when you want and with as much money as you want or need is to use an online retirement calculator. Here is the website of my favorite retirement calculator:

AARP Retirement Calculator (https://www.aarp.org/work/retirement-planning/retirement_calculator.html#!/about-you/marital-status)

With this calculator, you can estimate pension payments (if you have a pension), social security, your spouse's pension and social security (if you have a spouse), and any other income you may expect in order to help you estimate how much you need to save up on your own to retire when you want to retire with as much of an income as you want. You can even change retirement ages with this calculator to see how much you need to save to retire at different age ranges.

Keep in mind that 90 is now the estimated life span, so make sure in your calculations that you allow your money to last at least that long, and 67 is the new official retirement age.

For right now, and this is important, calculate how much you need to be putting in to retire at 67 with as much money as you think you'll need as a bare minimum. We are going to aim for earlier than

HOW MUCH DO YOU NEED TO RETIRE ON?

67, if you started investing early enough, but for now, we want to know the bare bones minimum amount you will need to put in in order to retire comfortably by 67.

When asked average return amount, just use 10%. This is what the market tends to average long term.

Here is a second calculator. It works a bit differently, but is also a good calculator. This calculator really allows you to change variables to see how it affects the amount of money you need to be putting in.

Calculator.net
(https://www.calculator.net/retirement-calculator.html?cagenow=24&cretirementage=60&clifeexpectancy=85&cstartingprinciple=300&cannualaddition=0&cmonthlyaddition=300&cinterestrate=30&cinflationrate=3&x=101&y=12)

Once you have figured up your goal, that is, how much money you need to save monthly in order to retire at least by 67 with the bare minimum amount of money you wish to retire on, you now make this amount a bill that you pay every week, every two weeks or every month. It is a bill that you pay as if it were a utility bill or a car payment. Come Hell or high water, you pay that amount to your Retirement Fund. It is non negotiable. You can pay weekly, every other week or monthly, whatever is easiest for you. But pay every time.

There are three things you can do to really speed up how soon you can save up a nest egg big enough for retirement. The first thing you can do is start investing when you are young. The second is to start investing when you are young. And the third is to start investing when you are young. It is really that important! Make it a priority while you are young. Unfortunately, most people don't get any financial common sense until much later in life. I include myself here. You wouldn't believe how much of a difference it makes to start investing early. Time is the currency of currency. The longer the length of time you have your money invested, the more it keeps doubling. Compound interest is evidently one of the most powerful forces of this world.

If you are reading this book and you are no longer young, all is not lost. I just really want to emphasize to the younger crowd how easy all this becomes if they start early.

SETTING UP YOUR RETIREMENT FUND

Let's take that money you are now ready to be putting away *consistently*, like a bill for your retirement, and put it somewhere it can grow.

Remember that what I'm about to tell you is my opinion. It is what I do myself. But neither I nor anybody else can promise you that you will never lose money or that what has worked in the past will work in the future. That being said, this is what I do with my own money, which tells you how much I believe in what I'm about to say.

I have chosen TD Ameritrade for my retirement fund. I actually chose Scottrade, but TD Ameritrade bought Scottrade out. If you have another online brokerage account you prefer that is fine. I simply use TD Ameritrade and know how to tell you to use it so that is what I'm suggesting. To open an account, go to www.TDAmeritrade.com. If you have trouble, call them at (800) 669-3900 if you are in the US. For those of you outside the US, use (800) 368-3668. I have no affiliation with TD Ameritrade, and make no money when you open accounts with them.

When you make payments to your Retirement Fund, TD Ameritrade is where you will be sending your money. Remember, just putting your money into TD Ameritrade doesn't mean it is invested. When you put money in there the money is simply sitting there. It doesn't go into an investment until you place an order to buy a specific investment. We will go over that shortly.

Some people are afraid of doing their own investing; they have heard horror stories of other people playing with stocks and losing a lot of money, or something similar. What we are doing is going to be different, so don't fear. And don't freak out when you send your first check to TD Ameritrade. The money is not invested until you place an order. Also, TD Ameritrade does not charge anything until you place orders. They even pay a little interest on the money you have in their accounts that is not tied up in an investement. There may be a minimum balance requirement though.

One more thing I'd like you to do is to go to www.StockCharts.com and get familiar with playing with stock charts. For now, just get familiar with looking at stock charts on these sites. A little later I'm going to teach you how to read the charts in a very simple way. All the charts I am using will be from www.StockCharts.com. I used to use Yahoo's free chart service, but they changed it too often and too much for me. I also used Big Charts quite a bit, but they would not give me permission to use their charts in this book. For this reason, I now prefer www.StockCharts.com, which is a great site, with friendly people.

PENSIONS

If you have a pension, an IRA, or anything similar then this is going to make up the bulk of your Retirement Fund. With most of these programs, your employer matches how much you put in (up to a point). That means if you put in $100, they put in $100. That is doubling your money every time you add to your retirement. You just can't beat that. Its free money, and better than any return in the market. And its also protected from predators. So if you have a pension, maximize it. This will make up the bulk of your retirement fund.

If you are self employed and do not have a pension, like me, or your pension is not going to be enough to allow you to retire at 67 with as much money as you want, then you are going to have to do the rest on your own. Even some of the largest companies no longer have good retirement programs.

In either case, when you used the online retirement calculator, it took into account any pension, social security, and other possible income and then came out with an amount you need to be putting aside. If you do have a pension, it may be a small amount (or none at all) that you need to be saving. If you do not have a pension, or a small one, the amount you need to put aside may be much larger.

YOUR RETIREMENT BILL

Remember, the first thing that you are going to do is to determine how much money you need to set aside to retire, at a bare bones minium, at age 67, with as much money as you think you need to be comfortable. You are going to pay that amount as if it is a bill, sending it to TD Ameritrade or another online brokerage of your choice. This is a bill to yourself. Your retirement bill.

If you have a pension, you may need to put in very little, or you many not even need to put any extra in at all. If you do not have a pension, you may need to put in quite a bit. Either way, this money must be treated as a bill.

I know I am repeating myself quite a bit, but there is a saying that a person needs to hear something new seven times before they hear it once.

BUFFETT WINS A BET!

In 2007, Buffett made a bet for $1 million that a simple, passive (unmanaged) index fund would outperform an investment fund that was actively managed by "experts" who charged a lot of money for their services. The bet was to last 10 years, and all proceeds were to be donated to a charity of choice.

An index fund is simply a fund that follows one of the stock market "indexes", like the DOW, the S&P 500, or the NASDAQ. Nobody is "managing" the fund, the fund is simply made up of the stocks of that particular index.

A managed fund is where a person, or persons, actively buy and sell stocks in an effort to do better than the indexes. In exchange for their services, they charge fees.

Buffett won the bet, big time.

The index fund Buffett chose, a simple S&P 500 index fund, over the ten year period, averaged a growth rate of 7.1% compounded annually, while the managed fund only gave an average return of 2.2%.

In overall growth, over the 10 years of the bet, the index fun grew 99%, while the expert's fund grew only 24%. This means that a simple index fund, with low to no fees, that anyone can buy on their own, did almost 4 times better than a fund actively managed by a highly paid expert.

Almost everyone I talk to wants to *predict* the next big stock. Or they want me to predict the next big stock, like these fund managers claim to be able to do. But it is next to impossible.

For the conservatively invested Retirement Fund, we are going to take Buffett's advice and look at index funds.

THE CONSERVATIVE RETIREMENT FUND

For the bare bones Retirement Fund, I invest a bit more conservatively than I do with the Accelerated Retirement Fund that you will learn about in a minute. Remember, the conservative retirement fund is the fund we calculated as a bare bones minimum to retire by 67 with the amount of money you simply have to have. For those of you with a pension, your pension may cover part or even all of this fund. For those of you whose pension does not cover it all, or who have no pension at all, this fund is where you will invest conservatively. We are trying to at least guarantee a good, comfortable retirement with this fund. With the Accelerated Retirement Fund, which we will go over soon, we will try to speed up retirement so that you may be able to retire earlier, and increase the amount you can retire on.

I used to recommend BRK-B (Berkshire Hathaway) for the conservative retirement fund. This is Warren Buffett's company, and boy does that man know how to make money. He is like the Michael Jordan of investing, and his fund has averaged well over 20% per year. That is over twice of what the overall market averages, and much more than most other money managers have been able to reach. But as of this writing, the man is 88 years old. Buffett says he has a successor in line that will do a good job, but you never know. I think it will be very tough to find anyone that will be able to match Buffett's record. I am currently still using BRK-B for my

Retirement Fund, and have for years, but as of right now, I just don't know whether to continue recommending BRK-B to new investors or not. I will leave that up to you.

Aside from BRK-B, what I now recommend for the Conservative Fund is to invest in simple index funds. My favorite is SPY, which is the S&P 500 index. This is the same index Buffett recommended in his bet.

To put it simply, in my opinion, I believe you should invest the money you are setting aside for retirement into SPY. Don't watch it. Don't try to time the market. Every time you get a decent amount of money saved up in your Retirement Fund, simply use it to buy more SPY. If you are not sure how to buy on TD Ameritrade, simply call them up and ask for help the first time or two. Every time you place an order with TD Ameritrade, it is going to cost you $7, so don't buy one stock at a time. Wait until you have saved up a decent amount to make the $7 cost worth your while. And if you do call them for help, be careful, they may try to talk you into using one of their brokers.

Divide the amount of money you have saved up (plus $7) by the price SPY is currently trading at, and that gives you the number of shares to buy. If you have $3,007 saved up, for example, and SPY is trading at $250 per share, then you would be buying 12 shares. ($3007 saved up, minus the $7 for fees, equals $3000 available. $3000 divided by $250 per share price gives you 12 shares you can buy).

When the price gets up pretty high, it will often go through a split that lowers the price, making it easier for the average person to buy. For example, if the powers that be were to split SPY right now, which is around $250 per share, they might do a 5:1 split, meaning that if you owned 1 share at $250, after the split you would own 5 shares at $50 each. A 5:1 split is pretty big, and unusual, but you get the basic idea. Most people can afford to buy $50 dollar shares easier than they can buy $250 shares, so even though the amount invested is the same, the market tries to keep the prices low enough that the average person will remain interested.

If you ever look at your portfolio and overnight it seems crazy off, it is most likely that your investment has gone through a split that TD Ameritrade hasn't accounted for yet. For example, if you had 1 share of SPY at $250, and the next day, you have 1 share at $50, the price has split but the split has not been corrected in the system yet. This has only happened to me about twice in 20 years, but it is a shock if you don't know what happened. I just call up TD Ameritrade and ask them if the fund went through a split, and how long before Ameritrade fixes the balances. Sometimes it takes up to a week for TD Ameritrade to get everything straightened out.

ACCELERATING RETIREMENT, ACCELERATING WEALTH

We now know how much money we need to be setting aside in order to retire, at a minimum, by age 67, with an adequate amount of wealth. All else fails, you are now covered. You are building a safety net. If nothing else, you will at least be set to retire by 67 with enough money. Now that we have a safety net in place, we are going to try to accelerate that retirement age and increase the amount of money we will have to retire on.

We are already sending a certain amount of money to TD Ameritrade, or whatever your online brokerage of choice may be, as a bill towards our retirement fund. Now we are going to learn to handle our money in a way that may leave us a little extra to put into our retirement fund on a regular basis in hopes of retiring earlier than 67, and with more money. And with this money, we are going to invest pretty aggressively.

Let me repeat: the bulk of your retirement will be coming from your pension, or if you don't have a pension, from more conservative investments. This is your safety net. With any extra money we put in, we are then and only then going to swing for the fence.

Critics of my method in the past have claimed that it was too aggressive. The aggressive part is only suggested as a topping or an add-on to a much more conservatively managed base Retirement Fund.

FINDING MORE MONEY TO INVEST

We need to find a way to manage our money so that we know how much we make, where it all goes, and hopefully have enough at the end of each paycheck to send at least a little extra to our retirement fund in order to accelerate the growth of our money tree. I know money management sounds tedious and boring, but if you do not master the handling of your money, it won't matter how much you make or don't make, you will always have money troubles. I don't care how rich or poor you are, you will always be able to spend more than you have if you are not prudent.

I would like to recommend the works of Dave Ramsy and YNAB (https://www.youneedabudget.com/). Both of these methods teach ways to track every penny you make, and to create categories of where your money goes, along with budgets for each category. YNAB is espeically handy because it is a software program where you give every single dollar you make a job. When you get paid, you go ahead and assign each dollar a job so that you know exactly where you stand. You deposit your paycheck and immediately assign a certain amount of that money to pay the electric bill you know is coming, a certain amount for rent, and so on. With this method, you simply need to find a way to spend less money frivilously so that you can have a little extra money to send to your retirement fund every month. There are several other money management systems out there. Do a search and find one that best fits you.

FINDING MORE MONEY TO INVEST

Though I like Dave Ramsey and YNAB, I do things my own way. The method I use to manage my money is very simple: I use quicken software. Each time I get paid I put the money into my checking account. I then pay for any necessities I have, like water, electricity, groceries- anything I have to have to survive I go ahead and pay it. When I get done paying bills, I see how much money I have left from that check. Whatever money is left over after paying true necessities, the things I have to have in order to survive, is divided up into three slush funds: a Fun Fund, a Big Fun Fund, and a Retirement Acceleration Fund.

Any time I want to buy something that is not a necessity, like clothes, a snack, a new tool, or even chewing gum, it comes out of my Fun Fund. If I don't have any money in my fun fund, I can't buy anything that is not a necessity. The big fun fund is for vacations. The retirement acceleration fund is for (1) Paying off credit card debt and then (2) savings and (3) trying to retire earlier than the base age of 67, and with more money.

If you are married, this way of handing money can really reduce money angst. Each of you has a Fun Fund. If you want something, and you have money in your Fund Fun for it, then you can buy it. If you don't have enough money in the Fun Fund, then you cannot. Its as simple as that. The same goes with your spouse.

Many couples fight because they feel the other is spending too much money on frivolous things. With this method, you each have your own fun money with which to buy whatever you want, whenever you want it, provided you have enough money in the Fun Fund to do so. If she wants a new dress, she can get it, as long as she has enough Fun Money. If he wants a new knife, he can get it, as long as he has enough Fun Money. No bickering over what the other buys.

Each person's Fun Money is theirs to do with as they wish. But you can't spend more on fun than you have in your Fun Fund. No credit, no getting into debt, not even with yourself. From now on, however much Fun Money you have is simply how much Fun Money you can spend. If you don't have enough Fun Money, you need to save up, make more money or cut your necessities.

This way of managing your money becomes a game. When you see that the less you spend on your bills the more money you have for buying fun things, the more you want to live frugally. You will want to cut costs so that you will have more Fun Money to do and buy things with.

Most people get in credit card debt because they buy things they want in excess of what the amount of money they have. That will have to stop. By using this method, you become less likely to impulse buy, purchasing things you don't really want or need and regretting it later. Knowing you can only buy as much as the Fun Money you have will let you makes you more discriminant in what you purchase. You will get pickier. All of this happens over time though. At first you will resist using this method, because you are, like the rest of us, most likely addicted to buying. But over time, you get more and more into an understanding, and a rhythm, and then you really, really start liking the system. At least that has been the way it has worked with me and those around me that I have helped with the system.

If you seem to have no money left over after paying for necessities, then you may need to look at what you see as "necessities", or get a better job. The only ways to increase excess money is to decrease your living expenses, make more money, or both.

FINDING MORE MONEY TO INVEST

I usually use the following percentages for calculating fun money, etc:

30% of the excess money after paying bills goes to the cc debt/savings/early retirement fund. Lets say you have $100 left over. $30 goes to the Early Retirement Fund.

The remaining 70% is split between the Fun Fund and the Big Fun Fund. If you had $100 left over after bills, $70 goes to the Fun Funds ($35 to the regular Fun Fund and $35 to the Big Fun Fund).

If you have a spouse, the 70% ($70) that goes to the Fun Fund will be split three ways: $23 to each fund.

Quicken will allow you to "post-date entries". If today is November 14, 2018, I can enter my "slush funds" with dates far in the future, like November 14, 2028. This will allow you categories to enter your slush funds into. As you spend money from those slush funds, you reduce the amount in those funds on quicken by that amount.

Here is an example Quicken Register with post-dated slush funds:

Date	Num	Payee / Category	Memo	Payment Exp	Clr	Deposit	Balance
2/8/15		Netflix / TV		8.75			4,119.08
2/9/15		Deposit / Salary				322.25	4,441.33
2/9/15	v	Raceway / Car	gas	43.00			4,398.33
2/9/15	v	Jack's / Groceries		22.17			4,376.16
2/13/15		Deposit / Salary				628.77	5,004.93
2/13/15	v	Kroger / Car	gas	24.00			4,980.93
2/14/15		Farm Bureau Car Insurance / Car Insurance		127.00			4,853.93
2/16/15	v	Sunrise Market / Car	gas	46.68			4,807.25
2/16/15	v	Sunrise Market / Groceries		2.28			4,804.97
2/17/15		Hulu / TV		7.99			4,796.98
2/18/15	v	Walmart / Groceries		31.10			4,765.88
2/19/15	v	Kroger / Car	gas	15.00			4,750.88
1/28/21		CC, Debt, Savings, Early Retirement Fund / Slush Fund					4,750.88
1/29/21		A's Fun Fund / Fun Fund		35.00			4,715.88
1/30/21		B's Fun Fund / Fun Fund		50.00			4,665.88
1/31/21		Big Fun Fund / Fun Fund					4,665.88
5/20/15	Num	Payee / Category	Memo	Payment Exp		Deposit	

Current Balance: 4,750.88   Ending Balance: 4,665.88

Reprinted with permission © Intuit Inc. All rights reserved.

Notice that the bold line denotes today's date. There are example slush funds under the bold line for "CC, Debt, Savings and Early Retirement" (more on that in a minute), "Spouse A's Fun Fund", "Spouse B's Fun Fund" and a "Big Fun Fund". Whenever you get more "Early Retirement Money" or "Fun Money" you just add that amount to the slush funds you already have. Whenever you send a check in to invest from your "Early Retirement Fund", or spend "Fun Money", you simply deduct that amount from the correct slush fund. Easy.

PAYING OFF DEBTS and CREATING A SAFETY NET

Before we use the Early Retirement Money we just learned to calculate for accelerating retirement, I think it best to use it to pay off debts and save up an emergency cash reserve. You don't have to, but I think it is best. I know this is frustrating- you probably want to skip to adding more to the retirement fund, but by doing it the way I am showing, we first build a bare-bones retirement investment that is working for us, we end up debt free, and we end up with cash reserves for emergencies. Once those things are set up, you are financially on solid ground and you can start trying to accelerate your retirement.

If you start trying to accelerate your retirement before all those things are set up, or try to risk too much with your Retirment Fund, a set-back could be rough. But if you have your financial feet on solid ground, you can tolerate a bit more risk without having to worry about a setback being the end of the world. In other words, secure your survival first, then go for the fence. Don't go for the fence before your survival is secured. Also, never risk your basic retirement on aggressive investing. You only go after the riskier investing with the excess money we learned to calculate in the last chapter.

By saving up a cash emergency fund, in an emergency, we won't need to borrow money from a credit card or other lender that is going to eat you alive with interest. This is what most people do, and they end up getting behind and going deeper and deeper into the hole. This is what credit cards want you to do. They want you to get behind and never catch up. This way they loan you money once or twice, and you end up paying them for it for life. You become THEIR money tree. They loan you a small amount, but in the end get paid back WAY more than they ever loaned you. We are trying to work our way to doing the reverse: earning money once, but spending it for life. We want to create our own money tree.

We want to pay off those credit cards and other debts (aside from our mortgage and / or student loans- more on that in a minute) with the Accelearated Retirement Fund money. Once that is done, we want to funnel that money into building up a decent savings account that you can borrow from if you ever have an emergency. This way you are borrowing from yourself in times of emergency. Not only will you borrow from yourself interest free, but you will also be making money on your savings if you park the money into a money market account. You will have become your own bank from which you can borrow when needed. This is much better than borrowing from a credit card and falling into their black hole from which it is hard to escape.

So here is the order so far:

1. We have calculated how much money you need to pay yourself each month to retire comfortably at age 67 with the bare minimum you want to retire on. This is your Retirement Fund, and you pay it as a bill. For some of you, your pension may cover some or all of this fund.
2. We are going to invest this money in SPY.

PAYING OFF DEBTS AND CREATING A SAFETY NET

3. We have also started keeping up with our bills better. We keep up with our incoming money versus our necessities. What is left over is our excess money. We split the excess money between Fun Money and an Early Retirement Fund, which we are going to use to try and expedite our retirement.
4. Before we start investing the Early Retirement Fund Money, I think it best to use the money to pay off our debt and build savings.
5. The only exceptions to paying off debts first is your house Mortgage and Student Loans. If you wait until those huge loans are paid off you'll be waiting too long before you can begin to invest strongly. So just include those payments as bills and don't worry about trying to pay them off early.
6. Once debt is paid off, funnel the Early Retirement Fund Money into building a savings account. To be safe, build up enough money to live off of for three, six or nine months, depending on how cautious you want to be.
7. Once your savings account is big enough, then it is time to funnel the Early Retirement Fund Money into accelerated investing, which we will go over next. The goal now is to try to speed up your retirement age.

Once again, I want to point out that starting early is HUGE. Unfortunately, most people, like me, don't get enough sense to invest until much later in life. Then it becomes much slower and harder. If you start young you can retire young. And believe me- you want to!!

THE AGGRESSIVE, EARLY RETIREMENT FUND

Let me say, one more time (yes I realize how repetitive I am being), that the Retirement Fund is a conservative investment with which we are trying to guarantee a decent retirement. The aggressive investing I am about to go over is to be added to the conservative base. We are trying to guarantee our financial future first, and then swing for the fences once we know that is secure.

For my aggressive investing, I have found over many years of trial and error, that it is best, first of all, to find investments that have a very long track record of being in an uptrend, that also have a good track record of paying dividends. In this way, we are making money two ways: (1) we are making money as the investment rises, and (2) we are making money off the dividends of the investment. If the investment ever dips, it is easier to hold out (if you need to) knowing that you are still making money off the dividends. I simply keep track of this collection of investments that meet these two criteria, and invest in the ones that are moving up the fastest. I am therefore in the fastest rising of the most predictably uptrending investments, that also usually pay good dividends.

In the past, I used to simply invest in investments that were moving up the fastest. I didn't care if they had a long track record of being in a constant uptrend, or if they paid dividends, I just wanted the fastest rising ones. The problem turned out that stocks with unpredictable patterns sometimes made you money and sometimes lost you money. They were very unpredictable. But by investing instead in only those stocks that were in constant uptrends, the results became much more predictable. Nothing in life, and definitely nothing in the stock market is certain, but there are definitely higher and lower probabilities. We are simply trying to align ourselves with the highest probabilities.

Below is a graph of BRKB.

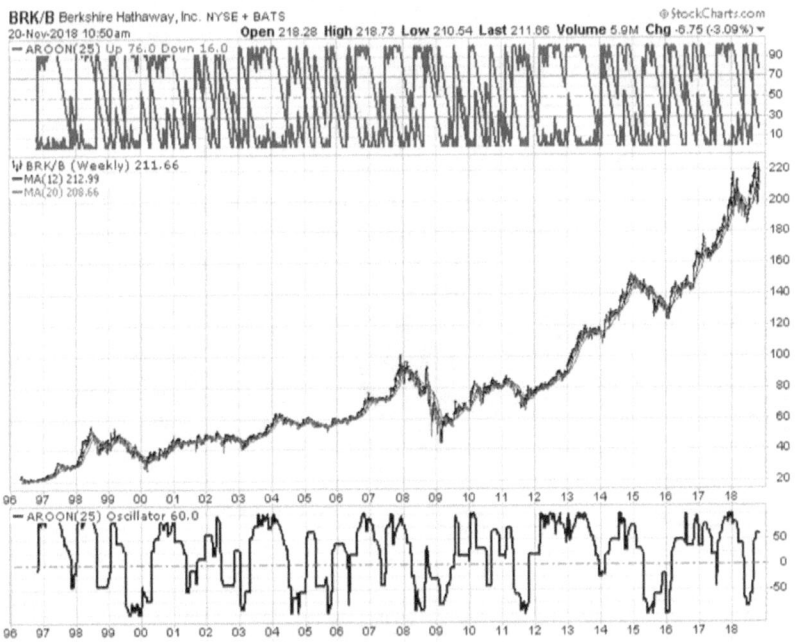

Graph courtesy of StockCharts.com

Notice that since 1996, the longest we can look back, BRK-B has been in a constant climb… in a constant overall uptrend. Yes, it's a little jerky, a little "stair-steppy", but that is just how the market moves. There are no straight lines, but overall, BRKB-B has been in a continual uptrend. Nothing is certain, but all things being equal, if the stock has been going up (overall) since 1996, and it is now

2018, 22 years later, then there is a good probability that it will keep going in that direction for the near future. Again, nothing is certain, but there is a good probability here. The odds are good, making it a safer bet.

Below is UNH, another investment on my list. Notice how it has not only been in a continual, long-term uptrend, but seems to have accelerated. I am saying this stock can never turn around and break into a downtrend. All I am saying is that when you are building a portfolio, filling it with a handfull of the fastest rising investments from a list of stocks that have continually, predictably only gone up has a much higher probability of making you good money than filling that portfollio with investments that are very unpredictable. Stocks that have continued in the same direction for decades tend to keep going in that same direction.

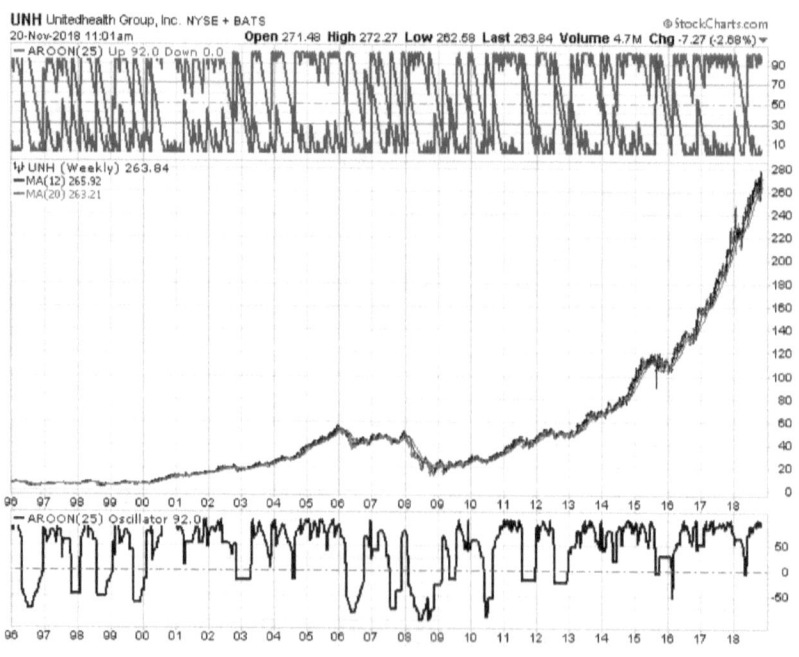

Graph courtesy of StockC/harts.com

Now compare the nice, continual uptrends of BRK-B and UNH above with the two graphs below, LNG and AMD.

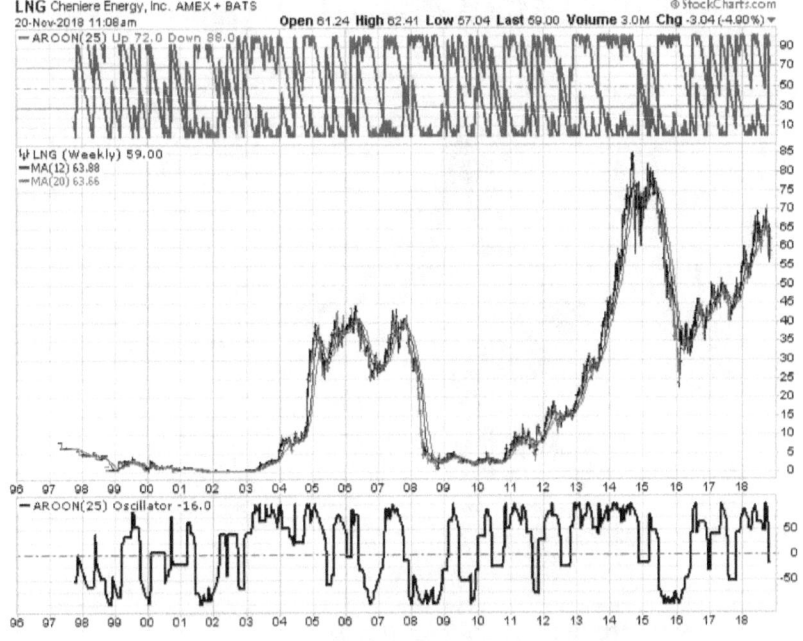

Graph courtesy of StockCharts.com

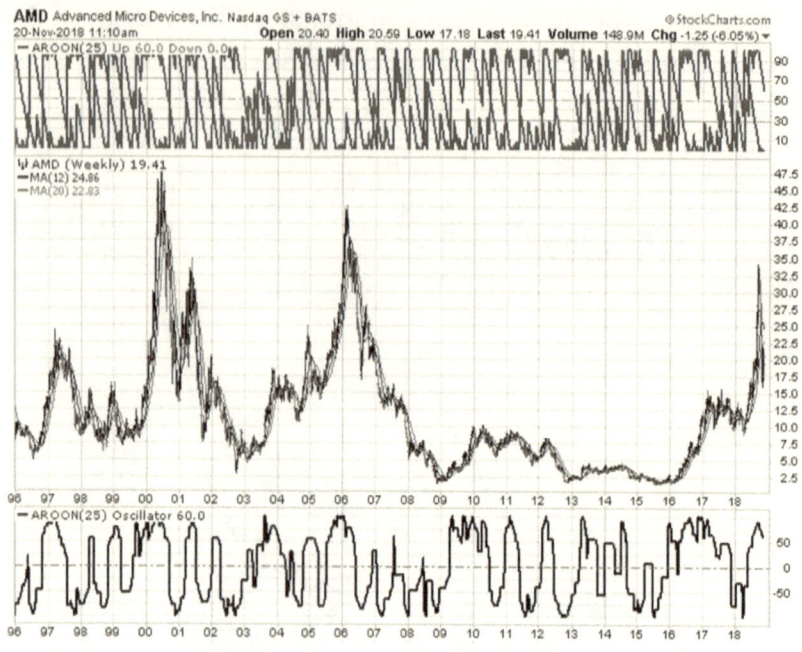

Graph courtesy of StockCharts.com

Notice how unpredictable their patterns are.

If LNG or AMD starts rising nicely, and you try to jump in, the probability can go either way. There is just as good a probability that the investment will drop after you get in as there is a probability that it will go up more. This makes it hard to sleep at night, let me tell you. Predictability is much better. Though, again, there is nothing completely predictable in life or the markets, there is just more probable and less probable. Since I have switched to more probable investing, it has been much easier on me emotionally, and much more profitable.

As a side note, I used LNG and AMD as examples because I did a search for "hot stocks" and these two were highly recommended. See what I mean about not listening to the "experts" on tv?

THE AGGRESSIVE, EARLY RETIREMENT FUND LIST

The following is my current list of investments that meet my criteria of long term uptrends and usually good dividends as well.

Keep in mind that from time to time an investment will break its uptrend, and I will kick it off the list. Again, these stocks are so much more predictable than most other stocks, but from time to time even some of these will fall off. This is why you invest in several at a time. It is so seldom that one of these breaks its uptrend, that by investing in several instead of only one or two, if one you are in breaks out, which is rare, it is not a big deal.

From time to time I also find new investments to add to my list.

Here is my current list of 32 stocks that meet my criteria that I monitor:

AAPL, ADBE, AMZN, AWK, BIP, CL, CLX, DHR, DLR, GOOGL, HD, JNJ, KMB, KO, LANC, LMT, MCD, MKC, MMM, MSFT, NOC, PEP, PSA, RTN, STZ, TRV, UHT, UL, UNH, V, VVC, WM.

THE AGGRESSIVE, EARLY RETIREMENT FUND LIST, part 2

Once you get more experience, and if you are bold enough, I have a second focus for my Early Retirment Fund. One that can speed up results even more, but these recommendations may not be for the faint of heart- leveraged ETFs.

Leveraged ETFs are a secret niche I have found. They are not unheard of, but most people have never been exposed to them, or have any idea how lucrative they can be.

Leveraged ETFs is also an area that I received a lot of criticism from in earlier versions of my book- mostly from mainstream, academic investors. I'll address their concerns in a minute, but first let's go over exactly what an ETF is.

An ETF is an Exchange Traded Fund. They are like Mutual Funds in that they are a group of investments instead of one stock, but they don't have the fees or restrictions that Mutual Funds usually have. SPY, the index fund I recommend for the Conservative Retirement Fund, is an ETF.

If I ever refer to an ETF as an Electronically Traded Fund instead of an Exchange Traded Fund, please try to ignore it. I am a doctor and insurance companies are beginning to pay us with EFTs (Electronic

THE AGGRESSIVE, EARLY RETIREMENT FUND LIST, PART 2

Fund Tranfers). I talk EFTs all day long at work, and sometimes accidentally get my verbage mixed up when talking about the two different entities- ETFs (Exchange Traded Funds) and EFTs (Electronic Fund Transfers).

There are ETFs made to mimic the S&P 500, the Dow Jones Industrial Average, the Nasdaq, the markets of other nations, the Gold Market, the Silver Market, and just about anything else you can think of. Unlike Mutual Funds, you can buy and sell ETFs as easily as you can a stock or bond. The creation of ETFs was good enough to make me happy, but then the powers that be did something I really like- they created double and triple leveraged ETFs.

A leveraged ETF is an ETF that is "leveraged"- it goes up and down faster than the basic ETF. A basic S&P 500 ETF for example, like SPY, might go up 10% per year on average. But its double leveraged cousin goes up twice as fast. Its triple leveraged cousin goes up three times as fast. In 2014, TQQQ, which is a triple leveraged Nasdaq ETF, went up around 70%! Of course, leveraged ETFs go down faster too, so you have to know when to get out, or have a strong stomach during down years. We'll be going over that shortly.

Leveraged ETFs are able to dramatically increase price movements by using financial derivatives and debt to amplify returns. If that sounds complicated, it is. Some people believe that you shouldn't invest in anything you don't understand. I agree to a certain degree. If someone wants me to invest in land and I don't know them or understand the deal- no way I'm going to do it. However, in the market, I don't need to understand every detail of every company or investment I invest in. I really only want to know if it is safe (not an unregulated investment that might go out of business) and if it is going up in a way I can capitalize and make money on. Fundamental investors will disagree with me. That is ok. I have respect for fundamentalists, I simply have my own way of doing things. I am currently up over 87% on UNH, yet I know nothing about the company. I made a really good return on a Latin America ETF a few years back, yet I know nothing at all about their economy.

The speed to which leveraged ETFs go up and down is the main reason for the criticism I received in an earlier version of my book on this investing method. And there is truth to it. Mainstream investment wisdom considers Leveraged ETFs to be dangerous and not at all for the beginner. If you use them at all, it is only supposed to be over the course of a few hours, or a day- you are not supposed to hold onto them for months or years. Even the mainstreamers are beginning to change their tune about leveraged ETFs, but it is true that leveraged ETFs move FAST. If you are a beginner, I can't emphasize enough how aggressive leveraged ETFs are. Please papertrade first, then invest in regular ETFs, and once you feel comfortable you can start investing in Leveraged ETFs, if you want. In addition, leveraged ETFs are reset each day, so sometimes the ending price for the day is not the exact same as the starting price for the next day, which is one reason critics say not to hold onto them overnight. But those variations seem very small compared to the amount I have made on them. All I know is that they move fast, and I have made lots of money using them, once I figured out how to best invest in them.

I started out investing in Commodities. Commodities are bought on margin. Margin is where you pay just a fraction of the money down to own something much more expensive. For example, say you buy a house for $100,000 but you only have to put down $1,000 up front. If the value of your house goes up to $110,000 and you sell it, you

THE AGGRESSIVE, EARLY RETIREMENT FUND LIST, PART 2

just used $1,000 to make $10,000, which is an incredible percent return. This sounds great, and it is, as long as you *made* money, but the reverse is also true. What if you only had $1,000 to invest, and the value of your house dropped to $90,000. You just lost money- a lot, compared to what you put in. And you actually lost more than what you put in. This is where the term Leverage comes from. You are putting a fraction of money down, but making (or losing) the return on an object as if you had bought the entire object.

This is the way of things in the commodity market- you put down a small amount of money to control a much larger item. Let's say you pay $1,000 to control $10,000 in cotton. What happens is you pay the $1,000, and basically borrow the rest of the money from the brokerage firm. If the price of cotton goes up from $10,000 to $12,000 and you sell, you just made fast money, and a lot of it compared to what you put in. This is leverage. You put in a fraction of the total cost of the object but made the full return. But if the price drops $2,000, you just lost more than you put in. When or if this happens, the brokerage firm would do a "Margin Call", basically telling you that the $1,000 you put in has been used up and you need to pay more. Many times, the people in the commodity market that killed themselves in the past were for this reason- you can lose much more than what you put in. Many people got too risky and bought as much commodity futures as they had money for. Let's say they had $100,000 to their name and they invested it all, at margin. But if the market dropped a good amount, they may have ended up owing $500,000 on Margin Calls. It can be tragic.

This is why I switched to stocks. You cannot lose more money than you put in with stocks. You are not buying on margin with stocks. For me, the stock market is *much* slower paced and easier on the emotions than the commodity market. You tend to make slower returns but it is easier to deal with.

The reason I like leveraged ETFs so much is that you get somewhat close to the fast movement of a commodity, but it is still quite a bit calmer and you are not buying on margin. Your results are amplified, similar to a commodity, but you cannot lose more than you put in. Overall, leveraged ETFs have done me well. I like them very much. But again, if you are new, wade into them. Paper trade first, then do regular ETFs or a few stocks, and then work your way slowly into leveraged ETFs.

I think that the mainstream investors invest so conservatively that using leveraged ETFs scare them silly. But I was used to much scarier alternatives, so leveraged ETFs don't bother me much at all. Compared to the commodity market I was used to, leveraged ETFs are fairly mild and straightforward. Plus, I am only investing in leveraged ETFs with the second fund, the Aggressive Retirement Fund, after the first, Conservative Retirement Fund is set in place. I am swinging for the fences in this fund on purpose.

MY LEVERAGED ETF LIST

As with the stock list I mentioned earler, I am now only interested in monitoring leveraged index funds that have been traveling in an overall uptrend since its inception, or at least for many years. Again, nothing is certain, but it is more probable that a fund that has only gone up will continue doing so, at least for the near future. A fund with a scattered graph, on the other hand, is highly unpredictable.

Overall, the DOW, the S&P 500 and the NASDAQ, all American indexes, have been in an overall uptrend since inception- a very long time. There have been bumps in the road, but if you look at the overall, long term graph of each of these indexes, we have seen nothing but growth overall. This makes these funds a safe bet. Is there any such thing as a completely safe bet? No. But the probability is in our favor, much more so than if we try to predict a fund whose graph is all over the place.

Below is a graph of the S&P 500 since its inception. Notice that it has had bumps along the way, but has been in an overall uptrend the entire time. That big dip in the beginning area, by the way, is the Great Depression.

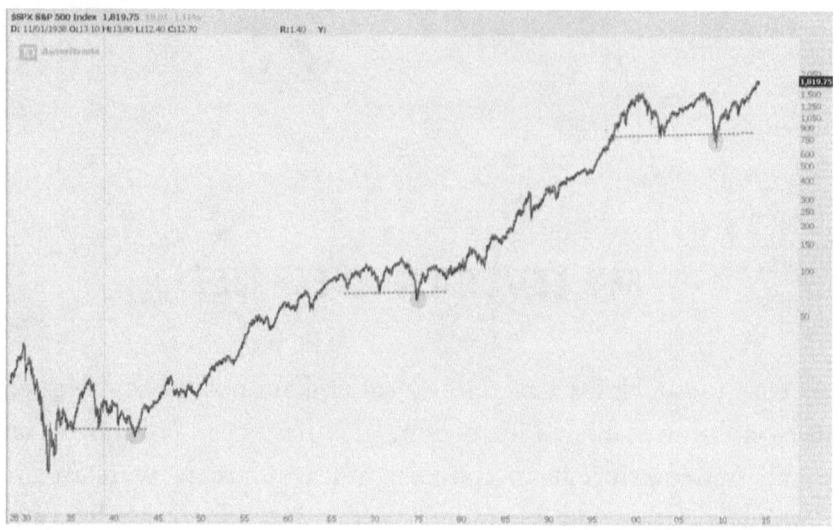

In the past, I used to monitor all leveraged ETFs in existence and get in the ones that were rising the fastest. It was a fast ride, a scary ride, and I both made and lost money regularly. I did well overall, but I do much better with the way I am now approaching these investments.

By limiting my leveraged ETF choices to just the DOW, the S&P 500 and the NASDAQ, I now have to watch only three funds, and I am simply choosing from the fastest rising of these very predictable funds (at least up to now). I make more money investing this way, and sleep very well at night.

Remember, it is best to paper trade first (that chapter is coming up), then start investing in non-leveraged ETFs until you get comfortable. Once you get comfortable you can move up to double leveraged ETFs (2x), then eventually triple leveraged ETFs (3x).

MY LEVERAGED ETF LIST

Here is a list of the leveraged ETFs that I follow- I personally follow the triple leveraged funds, but again, you may want to start out with non-leveraged funds first, then work your way up:

1. **DOW JONES INDUSTRIAL AVERAGE:**
   Non-Leveraged: DIA
   Double-Leveraged: DDM
   Triple-Leveraged: UDOW

2. **The S&P 500:**
   Non-Leveraged: SPY
   Double-Leveraged: SSO
   Triple-Leveraged: UPRO

3. **NASDAQ:**
   Non-Leveraged: QQQ
   Double-Leveraged: QLD
   Triple Leveraged: TQQQ

For me, I tend to invest almost soley in TQQQ now.

I have found that, for the most part, the DOW, the S&P and the NASDAQ all have very similar chart patterns, but the NASDAQ tends to move faster. So that's what I invest in- the NASDAQ, triple leveraged (TQQQ). That way I really only have to watch one.

THE FASTEST RISING

Now that we have a list of stocks to watch, and a list of leveraged ETFs, the next question is which ones to get into.

I really don't have a magic number of investments I want to be in. I don't have a set number of investments in my portfolio. I just don't want to be in only one or two, just in case one of them breaks trend. I tend to get in as many as there are that are going up nice and fast at the time. Many investments I am watching are in uptrends, but are going up very slow. I don't want them.

The way I keep up with the performance of these stocks and leveraged ETFs is with www.finviz.com.

As you can see in the screen shots to follow, I enter all the stocks and ETFs I want to watch into a watchlist on finviz. Then I can click on columns to rank which stocks or ETFs are performing the best over different time periods. I can rank the funds by best performing over a week's view, a month's view, a quarter's view, a half year's view, an entire year's view, or by year to date. This ranks for me, for each time period, the best performing funds, and will tell me how much they have risen in that specified time period. Just click on the time period at the top of each column you want the funds ranked in, and the software will rank them in order.

THE FASTEST RISING

Check out the following screenshots to see what I am talking about. Notice that both the stocks I mentioned earlier are on here, as are the leveraged ETFs. I really don't care which I get into, I just want to be in the funds (from that list of continually rising funds) that is rising the fastest.

I have DIA, SPY and QQQ on the list as well. These non-leveraged index funds are on the list mostly to compare my results to. For example, SPY is basically the S&P 500 (the one reccoemmended for the Conservative Retirement Fund). My goal is to beat it. I want my portfolio's overall return to be higher than the S&P 500, so I keep up with its returns.

Here are the screen shots:

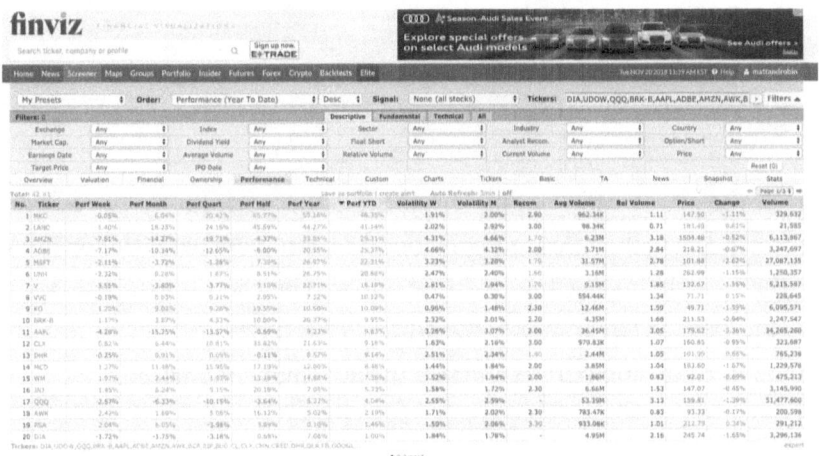

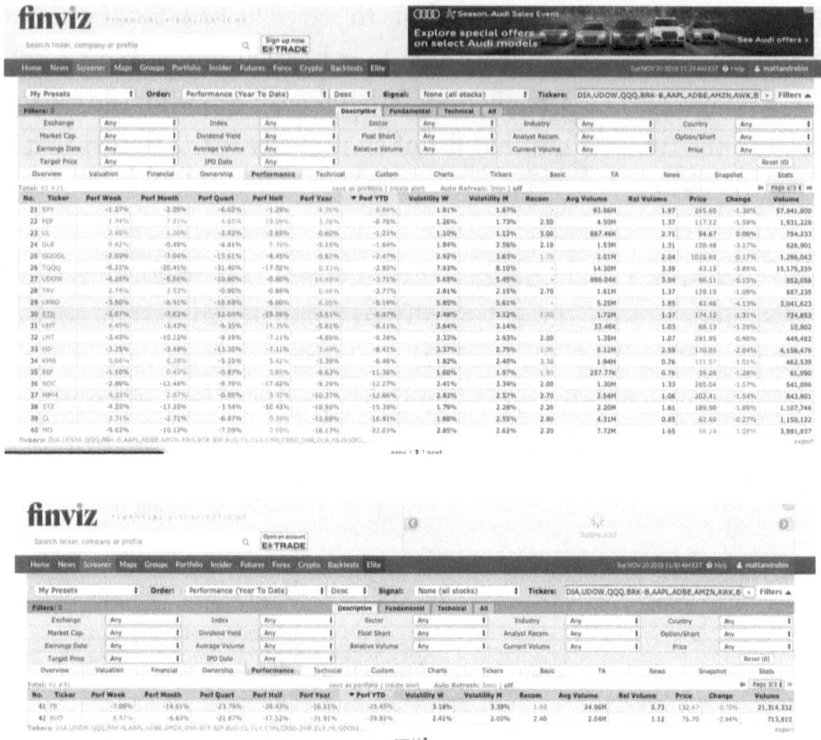

From the above list, I simply choose the top performing funds from that list. I usually take into consideration the best performing funds of the year, half year, the quarter, and maybe the month. A week is too short to interest me. A month may be too short too, unless the funds in that time period are also in the other time periods.

I look at the top 10 or so performing investments in each time period and usually choose the investments that are showing up over and over on each list, or almost on every list. For example, if TQQQ, ADBE, AMZN, V, MSFT, HD and UNH are showing up in the top ten of most of those time periods, those are going to be of most interest to me. They are most likely going to be the ones I choose. Being in the top ten of several time periods makes them not only the fastest risers, but also the most consistent, predictable risers on the list at that time.

I do not usually exit an investment unless it definitely breaks trend, or starts really underperforming other investments on the list. Which brings me to the emotional cycle of the market.

INVESTING IS EMOTIONAL

I cannot stress strongly enough how emotional investing is. We tend to be emotional with our money, not logical. At least in the beginning, you really need help (my newsletter), or at least start off paper trading, then trading very small amounts of money before putting larger amounts in.

Most people, as I said earlier in the book, enter a fund at the height of the excitement of a rising stock- they are experiencing the emotion of greed or hope. Yet such a run usually occurs right before it is about to fall back. When the inevitable drawback occurs, their excitement and greed and hope turns to fear and panic, and they typically exit the position, usually losing money in the process. Here is what this usually looks like:

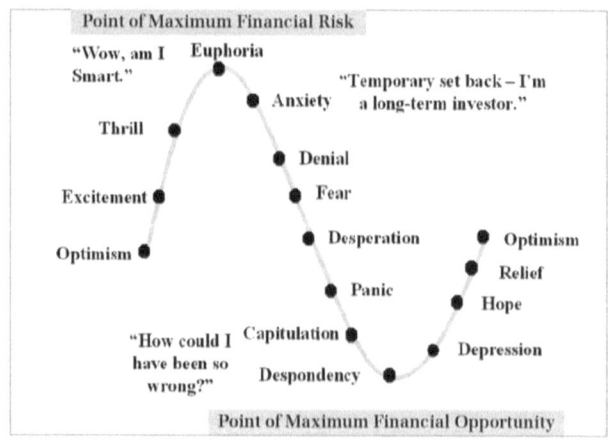

Now if you are investing in unpredictable stocks, this cycle is understandable. The average stock is so unpredicatable, you never know how long an uptrend will last, or how far it will fall when it breaks back downward.

But with our method of choosing more predictable stocks, we can more safely, more comfortably, follow a better investing method. We can get into a handful of the best performing stocks and ETFs that meet our criteria, and then when there is a drawback, which is just how the market works, we can add to our positions, thereby buying more at a lower price. Yes, if that stock ever breaks trend you may lose a little money, but think big picture. We are aiming at the most probable scenarios over years and decades. In the end, a small loss here or there doesn't matter much compared with the profits that tend to be made investing this way.

Look at BRK-B below. This is a five year chart. Notice that although BRK-B has always been in an overall uptrend, it hasn't gone straight up. It advances, draws back a little, advances, draws back a little- and it does this over and over and over. We all wish it would just go straight up and stop scaring us, but this is just how the market works.

The average investor gets in towards the peaks, when they get excited, and out in the valleys. But knowing that BRK-B has been in an overall uptrend for its entire existence gives us the confidence to do the opposite. We are going to get in, hold, and when there is a drawback, add to the position with any investing money we have saved up.

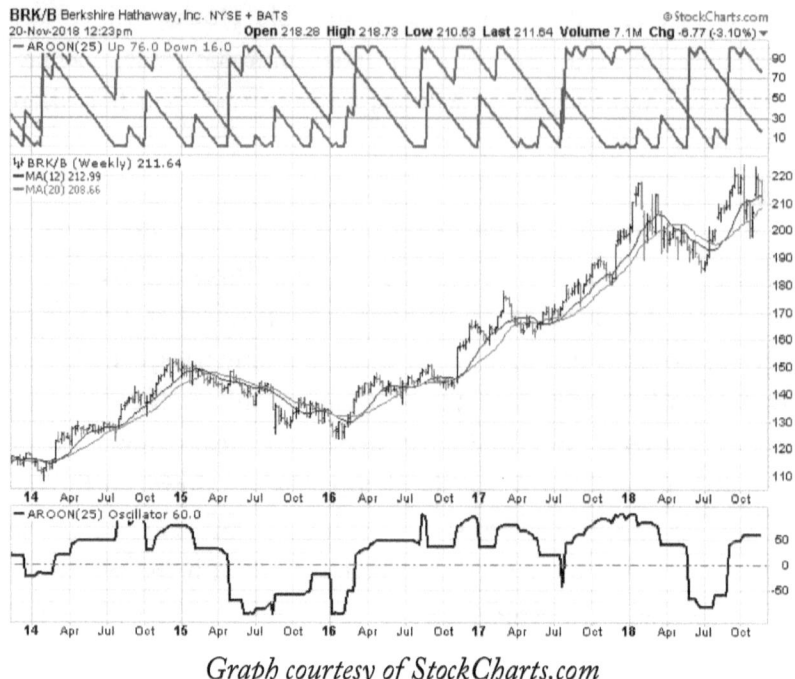

Graph courtesy of StockCharts.com

You may be starting to see why my newsletter is such a good idea. Yes, I am pushing my newsletter, both for me and for you. Investing is emotional, and counterintuitive. You have to be able to do pretty much the opposite of what everyone else is telling you to do, including the "experts" on television.

In my newsletter, I tell you what I am buying, what I am selling, when I am holding and when I am adding to an investment. 99% of my newsletters, which are emailed weekly, are me telling you "no changes". Seriously, it is that boring. But especially if you are new to the markets, it really helps to have someone to guide you and reassure you when the markets start to rock- for they will. This doesn't mean that if you get my newsletter that the clouds will part, the sun will break through and you will be rich overnight. It just means that I have been in this long enough that I have weathered most of the storms and, for the most part, know what to expect and how to react to most market reactions.

I cannot express this enough- investing is emotional, but needs to be approached logically, intelligently.

WHEN TO EXIT AN INVESTMENT

As I previoiusly mentioned. There are only two times I will usually exit an investment. (1) If it strongly breaks trend and (2) if it starts very much underperforming another stock on my list.

I don't try to predict. I don't listen to the television. I don't care how many people are screaming that an investment needs to be sold, I go by the two criteria above. Over and over and over "experts" try to predict what the market will do and what individual stocks are going to do. They are never right. Well, they are right the same percentage of the time as someone that is just outright guessing. In fact, years ago there was an experiment where a monkey throwing darts at a board with stock names pinned to it outperformed the best money managers out there. You cannot predict the market, you can only respond the most appropriately and intelligently to its tides- to its ebbs and flows.

Following is a graph of MO. MO was one of my favorite stocks for years. I used to include it in my Conservative Retirement Fund recommendations. MO averaged about 20% per year for a very long time. Unfortunately, the government changed a law with the tobacco industry (MO is a tobacco stock) that reduced investor confidence in the stock and it started to tank. So how do you know when to get out in a case like that? Looking at the following graph, in just viewing it can you not make out when the uptrend stopped and the

WHEN TO EXIT AN INVESTMENT

trend started going sideways, and then down? That is when you get out. If needed, you can draw an imaginary line over the peaks of the highs and under the valleys of the lows. When those two straight lines completely change direction, that is most likely a trend break.

Technically, when the graph dropped below the previous low, that is another good indicator to leave. See the low around October of 2016 of around $55 per share? This is called "support". Then see around April of 2018 how it broke below this price? That is a really good sign to get out. I had gotten in early enough that when I got out I left with a really nice profit.

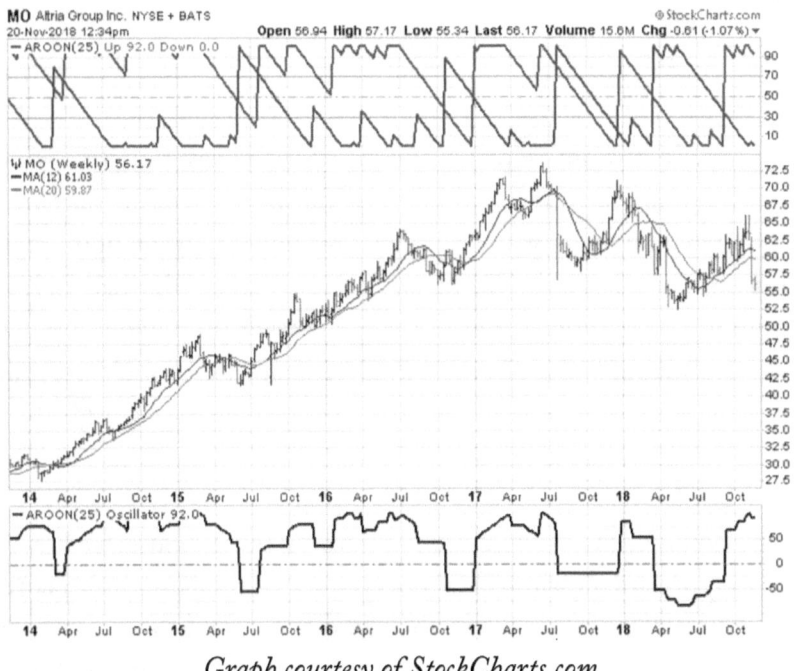

Graph courtesy of StockCharts.com

One more point. And this is important. When the market in general is doing ok, but a single investment tanks (breaks trend), it is time to exit that investment. But when the entire market sinks, and the individual investments are sinking pretty much in tune with the market, it is not, in my opinion, time to exit. The individual stocks are just mirroring the overall market. It is when an individual stock breaks trend out of tune with the market that there is trouble. Or if, when the market dips, a stock dips far more dramatically than the rest of the market.

The only exception to all of this is if you are right at retirement. If the market drops quickly and you are right at retiring, in my opinion, take your money and run. If the market seems to break trend, get out. I'm going to go over this idea in more detail in the next chapter.

I have confidence that the overall market, if it drops, will recover. But that recovery could take many years, depending on the size of the drop. If you are right at retirement, you may not have many years to wait for your portfolio to come back up- you may need the money now. So if you are right at retirement, in my opinion, I'd jump ship at a large drop. I know several retirees who had right at a million to retire on, but after a large market drop ended up with around a quarter of that amount. Eventually I feel their portfolio would have recovered, but they were needing the money right then, not five or ten years later.

In my opinion, the stock market is nothing but an emotional guage of the optimism, pessimism or uncertainty of the American people. When investors are confident, they tend to buy and the market goes up. This is due to the law of supply and demand- the more stock is bought, the less stock there is availiable, so it costs more per share. When investors are scared, they tend to sell and the markets drop, for the same reason- the more available the shares are, the less they are worth. When the public is undecided, some people are buying

WHEN TO EXIT AN INVESTMENT

and some are selling, so the market tends to go up and down over and over and over within a sideways channel.

You cannot predict the market. You can only respond intelligently to its movements.

NEARING RETIREMENT AND MY NEWEST EXPERIMENT

As previously mentioned, investing close to retirement is a little different. If the market goes through a small drawdown, it is no big deal, but if the market has a major correction, it could very much affect your nest egg, possibly taking years to recover- years you may not have if you are on the verge of retiring. I have seen this happen several times.

For this reason, we need a slightly different strategy when we get close to retirement. Before we get started with the "Nearing Retirement" strategy, there are three terms you need to know.

1. **Aroon** is a trend indicator that helps you to see whether a stock seems to be in a trend or not, which way the trend is going, and how strong the trend is. It also helps you to detect changes in trends.

    Aroon basically works by plotting out the number of days since a new high or a new low has been reached. The more new highs in a row, and the fewer the days between them, the stronger the evidence of an upward trend, and vice versa.

    A 25 day Aroon-Up, for example, is measuring the number of days since a 25 day high. A 25 day Aroon-Down,

NEARING RETIREMENT AND MY NEWEST EXPERIMENT

conversely, is measuring the number of days since a 25 day low.

2. The **Aroon Oscillator** plots the difference between the Aroon-Up (uptrend) and Aroon-Down (downtrend) indicators. It is another way to help you see trends and trend breaks.

3. **Moving Averages** average out the prices of the fund you are looking at so that you can see the overall trend better. It is the final method we are going to use to identify trends and trend breaks. Like the Aroon and the Aroon Oscillator, you must input the time period you want the price to be averaged out over. This will all make more sense in a minute.

In the following image, the Aroon indicator is placed above the stock chart. The green line is the uptrend indicator and the red line is the downtrend indicator. When the green line is above the red, it indicates an uptrend. When the red line is above the green, it indicates a downtrend. The closer the red or green line is to the top, the stronger that particular trend. The closer that line is to the bottom, the weaker that particular trend. When the two lines cross, it indicates a change in the trend. I have circled the areas where the trend changed on this chart of SPY, as indicated by a crossing of the lines.

Below the chart is the Aroon Oscillator. When the Oscillator line is above 0, it indicates an uptrend. When the line is below 0, it inicates a down trend. The closer the line is to 50, the stronger the uptrend. The closer the line is to -50, the stronger the downtrend. When the line passes down through 0, it is indicating a change from an uptrend to a downtrend. When the line passes up through 0 into the positive range, it indicates a change from a downtrend into an uptrend. I have circled the areas in the following graph where the trend changed according to the Aroon Oscillator.

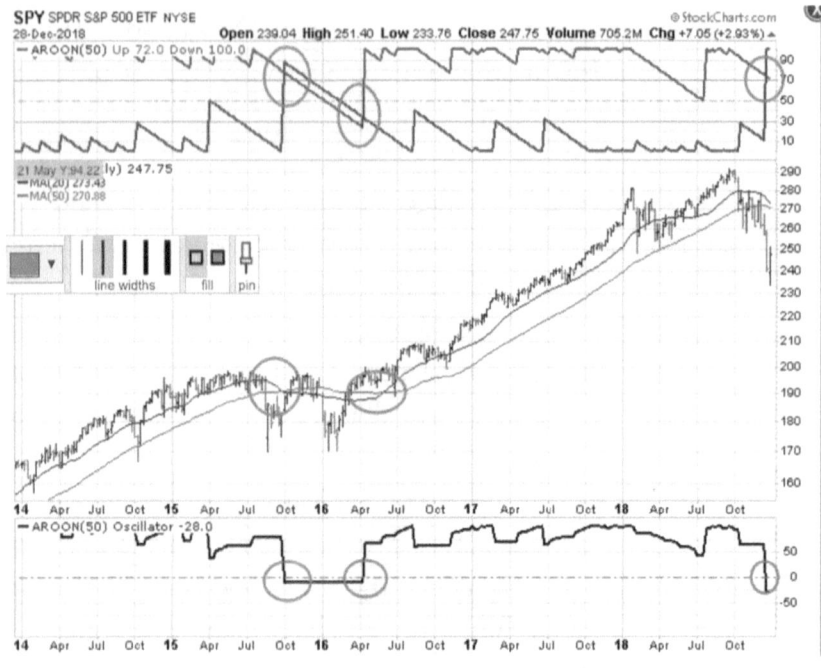

Graph courtesy of StockCharts.com

Lastly, the solid lines running almost on top of the stock chart are Moving Averages. Where the two Moving Averages cross tends to also indicate a change in trend. I have circled the areas where the Moving Averages indicated a trend change.

Notice that all three indicators tend to agree, for the most part, on the areas of trend breaks. In the final trend break, farthest to the right side of the chart, the Aroon and the Aroon Oscillator have both detected breaks, but the Moving Average has not- at least not yet.

I use three different indicators instead of just one in order to be more certain. If one indicator detects a break, but not the other two, I probably won't move. But if two, and definitely if all three indicators detect a break, it is a sign to take action.

You do have to play with the time periods of each indicator though until you find one that best "fits". If you use too short of a time period for your indicators, you would be getting in and out at every little crook in the stock price. If you use too long of a time period, you will never see a trend break and therefore never get out. So you have to play with the time period of the indicators until you get a "best fit" line for that particular fund.

In the previous 5 year chart of SPY, I used Moving Averages of 20 days and 50 days. With the Aroon and the Aroon Oscillator, I used 50 days. This information is entered into a box, like the one you see below, beneath each chart on StockCharts.com. You simply enter the indicator, the time period you want, and whether you want to view the indicator above or below the chart, then hit update.

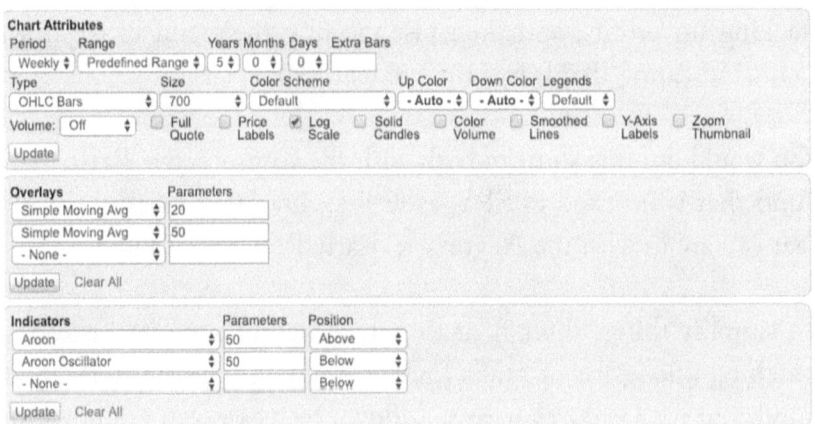

Most stocks you watch will need similar time periods for your indicators, but it is possible that not all funds you are watching will be best fit by the same time periods, so keep that in mind. In these cases, you will have to play with the time periods of the indicators to find the best fit for the past activity of that particular fund.

Now for the "Nearing Retirement Strategy"…

For the Conservative Retirement Fund, you are investing in SPY. Up until Retirement, you do not try to time the market, you just ride it. You don't even look at it, really. You have a set amount you are putting away and are simply adding that amount to your Conservative Retirement Fund regularly. It is as if that amount were a bill that you are paying to your future self.

But now, close to retirement, you start watching for trend breaks with the indicators above. In the example of SPY above, you would have gotten out at the first trend break, indicated by circles. The next circle indicates where it would have been safe to re-enter the market. Then there was another long ride up, where you were stacking up profits, and then just recently the trend broke down again, indicating that it was time to exit SPY again.

You would use this strategy both with the Conservative Retirement Fund that is invested in SPY, as well as any other stocks or ETFs that you are in with the Aggressive, Early Retirement Fund.

To simplify things though, at this stage (ie: retirement), instead of watching a long list of funds for the Aggressive, Early Retirement Fund, you may want to narrow it down to where you are investing in the manner just describe only in SPY. That way you are only watching one fund, a single one, and getting in and out at trend breaks, just in case.

If you are more daring and more confident in your investing skills, you could instead invest in a double or even triple leveraged ETF of the S&P, the DOW or the Nasdaq. But only do this if you have a lot of experience and are very confident in your understanind.

To refresh your memory, here is a list of the ETFs, unleveraged, double leveraged and triple leveraged, that track the major American indexes:

DOW JONES INDUSTRIAL AVERAGE:
Non-Leveraged: DIA
Double-Leveraged: DDM
Triple-Leveraged: UDOW

The S&P 500:
Non-Leveraged: SPY
Double-Leveraged: SSO
Triple-Leveraged: UPRO

NASDAQ:
Non-Leveraged: QQQ
Double-Leveraged: QLD
Triple Leveraged: TQQQ

If you become daring enough, you could even use this strategy before retirement. I'd still keep SPY as the Safe, Conservative Fund where you are trying to gurantee yourself a bare bones, minimum amount by the age of 67. I wouldn't try to time this fund, just let it ride like we mentioned earlier.

But with your Aggressive, Early Retirement Fund, where you are swinging for the fences with extra money, instead of tracking a long list of stocks and ETFs, you can simply use the above entry and exit strategy with only one double or triple leveraged ETF. My favorite is TQQQ, a triple leveraged Nasdaq ETF. It tends to move the fastest.

Again, the American indexes (S&P, DOW and Nasdaq) have been in a constant overall uptrend since inception. This does not mean that the American market can never faulter, but it does mean there is a good probability, especially when compared to other funds with unpredictable graphs, that it will continue to climb. This makes the indexes good, reliable funds to focus on. Instead of messing with handfuls of unpredicatable funds that go up, down and all over the place, you are tracking just one or two that are most likely going to keep climbing overall. You just get in and out as the indicators tell you to.

Keep in mind though that there is an IRS rule that if you lose money in an investment you can't get right back into that investment for some reason. There has to be a grace period, I think it is 3 months. So if you ever get in TQQQ for example, and it was a false start, and you lost a small amount of money, you can't just get right back in the next time the indicators tell you it is time. In that case, I'd switch to UPRO (the triple leveraged S&P fund) or UDOW (the triple leveraged DOW fund) for that run, switching back to TQQQ the next time.

False starts happen from time to time. The above example of SPY looks easy to spot, but sometimes you do get false starts. Sometimes you get a couple in a row. You simply follow the charts- get in when it says, get out when it says, and when the next big ride actually starts, you'll usually make up for any small losses you have incurred from the false starts, and then some.

Such a strategy, using only a single leveraged ETF for the Aggressive Fund is not for the faint of heart though, or for beginners. Get confident with your investing, get a bit of experience before trying that kind of strategy. I'm more and more using this strategy myself.

If you are not close to retirement, you could use this strategy not to get out of the market during downtrends, but to know when to best add to your positions during drawdowns.

I personally have my Conservative Retirement Fund invested in BRKB. (As I said before, Buffett is so old I don't know if I should continue to recommend you do the same or not. It is probably safer to invest in SPY for the Conservative Retirement Fund.)

Then, for my Aggressive Fund, I am investing in fewer and fewer funds. In fact, I am taking profits in most of my stocks and transferring the money to TQQQ. I am riding the waves of the market and add to my position during the drawdowns, right when the above indicators say that the trend is changing back to an upward climb.

CLARIFYING MY STRATEGY

Just so there is no confusion, the basic strategy I have been using is to:

1. Invest in SPY as the Conservative Retirement Investing Fund and simply ride the investment. I would not try to time it unless you are getting close to retirement. In that case, I would use the indicators from the last chapter to know when to exit and when it is safe to re-enter. Once in retirement, I would simplify the program by only investing in SPY, not bothering with the Aggressive Fund at all.
2. For the Aggressive Fund, I would invest in the fastest and most consistently rising funds out of the list of investments listed earlier in the book. These funds all meet the criteria of a constant overall uptrend and usually pay good dividends as well. Ride the market with these funds and add to your positions during the dips. Get out only during true trend breaks or if another fund starts to greatly outperform one you are in.

The following is the strategy I am playing around with to simply this method even further:

1. I am invested in BRKB (I suggest SPY for you) for the Conservative Retirement Fund. I pay into it like a bill and do not try to time anything.

2. For the Aggressive, Early Retirement Fund, I am looking at only being invested in one triple leveraged ETF at a time for my Aggressive Fund, using the above indicators to tell me when to add to my position after a drawback.
3. To be even more aggressive, one could use the indicators to get out during trend breaks down and in during trend breaks up, taking bite-sized chunks out of each upward run. I'm looking into that as well.

In the past, I would try to jump on whatever fund was starting to hit a good uptrend. It was frustrating, because by the time the fund showed up on my radar, it was well into the run and close to a drawdown. Sometimes I got in early enough to make a good profit, but a lot of the time I did not. And a lot of the time I was getting into very unpredictable funds, whith charts that were all over the place.

By only following TQQQ (and UPRO and/or UDOW if I ever take a loss on TQQQ), I am following a single fund that has been in a general, overall uptrend for over 100 years- very predictable, at least comparitively. Instead of jumping from one unpredictable investment to the next, and being late getting in, I can simply watch TQQQ and get in at the first sign of an uptrend, or at least add to my position then.

This is the strategy I am now testing.

FUNDAMENTALS VS TECHNICAL ANALYSIS

I'd like to address a few other points I've been criticized on in earlier versions of this book.

I am a big fan of Warren Buffett. I am a big fan for one reason- he gets great results. Buffett is a fundamental investor. For those of you that are new to the market, a fundamental investor is someone who studies every nook and cranny of a company before they buy stock in that company. They invest in a company only if they think the company is a very good company. This is one of the two main ways to make decisions in investing.

The other type of investor is a technical investor. A technical investor basically studies chart formations and uses indicators such as up-trends and down-trends to make investing decisions. Technical investors don't tend to study the company much at all. They feel that all they need to know about a company shows up in their stock chart. If a company is strong, prices rise. If a company goes weak, prices fall. I am more of a technical investor. I do look into a company a little bit to make sure they aren't going out of business or anything like that, but for whatever reason, I have always done best using mostly technical indicators. Many people use both fundamentals and technical indicators.

FUNDAMENTALS VS TECHNICAL ANALYSIS

I personally do not care, at all, whether a person is a fundamentalist or a technical trader. I use technical trading because it is what I do best with. However, it may not be what other people do best with, and that is fine by me. The only thing I care about is results. The fundamentalists and the technical traders are two opposing philosophies that tend to argue and butt heads constantly over which group is correct. I used to recommend Warren Buffett's company for the Retirement Fund but I personally use technical trading for my Aggressive, Early Retirement Fund. Several critics claimed that I was beiong hypocritical. They seemed to think I needed to pick one method and only one method.

As mentioned previously, years ago, there was an experiment in the markets where a few monkeys were given darts. These darts were thrown at a wall where the name of different stocks were listed. Whichever stocks the monkeys hit with darts were the stocks the researchers bought. In the end, the monkeys' investment portfolio did better than the top ranked analysts of the time.

Here is how much I don't care what method you use- only the results you obtain... if those monkeys continually beat the other guys, I may have used their choices. I only care about results, not the methods used to get them.

Buffett uses fundamentals, and he is an all-star at investing that way. But nobody else gets those results. Nobody. The fundamentalists always point at Buffett as proof that fundamental investing is the way to go, but that is not true. Buffett is simply very good at investing using fundamentals as a tool. Other fundamentalists don't do nearly as good. Other people use other tools and do well. Each person simply has to figure out which tool or tools they are best at using to go after the best returns. For me, I have always prefered to ride Buffett's investments for my retirement investing, and for my own investing, I have always done best with technical analysis.

PAPER TRADE FIRST

I've mentioned this many times, but if you are new to investing it really is best if you "paper trade" first. This goes mostly for the Accelerated Retirement Fund. With the regular, Conservative Retirement Fund, I'd simply go ahead and start buying SPY.

Additionally, once you are secure paper trading, you need to "wade in" to real investing bit by bit. Maybe invest first in stocks, and use very little money. Then maybe try a double leveraged ETF. Then work your way up to investing more and more money, higher and higher amounts, as you feel comfortable. Eventually you may be comfortable enough for triple leveraged ETFs, my favorite, and investing larger amounts.

There is a website that offers a free paper-trading account. I wish there was such a thing when I was beginning- it is a very good idea, and so helpful. Go to http://www.investopedia.com/simulator/ if you are interested (and I think you should be) and open a free papertrading account. You could also make a papertrading portfolio on www.finviz.com, which may be even easier.

With paper trading, you simply decide on the fund or funds you think you would invest in and then pretend that you bought some at the current price. Use the actual amount of money you would be investing. Figure out the number of shares you could buy, then "pretend buy" and enter them into your portfolio, either on investopedia or finviz. Be as realistic as possible. If you pretend you have a million dollars to invest, and invest tens of thousands of pretend dollars in dozens and dozens of funds, your papertrading is not going to realistically prepare you for the emotions of real trading where you may have much less money to invest, and can only afford a few shares of one or two different funds in the beginning. Be as realistic as possible.

Check your portfolio once per week or so to see how it is doing. As you save more money, pretend to buy more, and possibly different funds. Even after papertrading I like to create a "portfolio" on www.finviz.com to keep track of the funds I am really invested in. I find it simpler to understand and use than the one on TD Ameritrade. You do not have to do this though. TD Ameritrade, or whichever brokerage you use will also keep track of your portfolio. I just prefer finviz.

As you get going in your paper trading, notice how much patience it takes to invest. You will probably look at your papertrade portfolio several times a day at first, even though you don't need to. You will most likely get frustrated because it goes down, or it is not moving up very fast. Watching your portfolio for growth is like watching your child grow. If you stare at your child every second of every day you will not notice how much he or she is growing, but people that only see your child once or twice a year will be astonished every time they see your child. Even if your investments were to grow 100% this year, which is very unlikely, and even if that growth was constantly up (which never happens), that means it will only grow around 8% per month, which is around 2% per week, which is around .4% per day (Monday through Friday). So if you are watching it close, it will look like a snail crawling.

Not only that, but 100% in a year is huge- a very exaggerated example. Warren Buffett has been averaging, by my calculations, close to 30% per year. That comes to 2.5% per month, on average, .625% per week and .125% per day (Monday through Friday). You would really go nuts watching that portfolio grow, and it is an all-star portfolio!

When the portfolio grows, it tends to grow in spurts. So you will pull your hair out if you watch it too closely. The portfolio will stall, and seem to be going nowhere. Then it will drop a bit. It will scare you. You will want out. Then when it does go up, it tends to go up a chunk and you get happy. But then it stalls again, or goes down again.

Investing is a MENTAL game. You have to be mentally tough at first to be able to do it right.

Airline pilots are trained to look only at their instruments. Their instruments are always right. Sometimes things look weird when flying, or you get disoriented. If you try to fly by human decision-making, it can mean the death of you. So pilots are trained to trust their instruments no matter what. Only if the instruments fail are they to rely on their own decision making.

Investing is the same. We have a process. Use that process to make your decisions. If the stock stalls, or goes down a little, or the television says your investment is worthless, or your neighbor says you're going to lose your farm, you have to have the mental fortitude to "trust your instruments". Be a machine. Don't go by instinct or a "feeling". Use your instruments.

In any event, the purpose of this chapter was to tell you to paper trade first. First of all, if you are new to investing, there is some experience you need to gain, some wrinkles you need to smooth out before you take your hard earned cash and start aggressively investing it. You may think you understand things pretty well now, but I guarantee there are a few lessons waiting for you that only experience can provide.

The other reason to paper trade is to see how emotional investing can be. You need to pretend your own money is in the market, and watch how your emotions react to every fluctuation. When you can watch these fluctuations without letting your emotions get the best of you, without letting them take you over, so that your intellectual side can simply watch your instruments and make all your decisions based on the instruments, then you are ready for real money. But start small. Slowly increase how much you put in investments as you get mentally tougher and tougher. When you don't flinch at the fluctuations of your investment at the current level you have in, it is time to put more in. Eventually you will be all in.

Please do not rush this process though. This may be the most important chapter in the book. You have to be able to let your mind and emotions swing wherever they want, while you wait patiently behind the scenes, making the correct decisions logically, mechanically.

AFTER THE MORTGAGE AND/OR STUDENT LOANS ARE PAID OFF

Earlier I mentioned not including your mortgage or student loans as debts to be paid off before you start investing. If you wait until those are paid off you might be 80 before you start saving and investing. For those debts, just make your regular payments for now.

If you get to the point where you have enough money in your investments to pay those off, and are still on schedule for retiring early and with enough money, it is ok to pay those off early.

If you just make your regular payment to these two debts, and end up paying one off before you retire, "snowball" half of that payment into paying off the other debt. In other words, if you are paying $1,000 per month towards your mortgage and $1,000 a month towards student loans, and you pay off your mortgage, take $500 of that mortgage payment (half) and add it to your student loan payment of $1,000 making the total payment $1,500 per month. Let the other $500 "float" to pay your bills and end up making you more "Fun Money" and "Early Retirement Money". This way, you both accelerate becoming debt free, but you also reward yourself a bit.

Once both bills are paid off, "snowball" half of the total payment into your Retirement Fund or Early Retirement Fund and let the other half "float" like before. All investing and no Fun Money leads to a boring life. I don't understand the point in that. You should enjoy, but plan ahead as well. Split your money between the future and now. That's my opinion anyway.

I AM STILL LEARNING

I truly don't care which method I use in choosing investments, knowing when to get in and knowing when to get out. All I care about is results. If a method of investing works, I want to know about it. If a new method looks like it could be a good method, I try it out. More than that, if it does better for me than what I have been doing, I will switch to that method, or at least add it to what I am already doing.

One of the main points of this book is that you don't have to have advanced or fancy degrees in finance or investing to do well in the markets. Fundamentalists will most likely get angry over this statement. That is ok. They may do well using fundamentals. I have done well investing my Retirement Fund with Warren Buffett, who uses fundamentals. But in my own investing, I do best with technical analysis. This does not mean I don't respect fundamental analysis. Not at all. Some people do really well with it. I just do best with technical analysis for whatever reason.

Another of the main points of this book is coming up with very simple, very basic strategies for making good money. I did not name my books book Investing 101 and Investing 201 because I wanted it to be an academic introduction to all the fancy terms and strategies used in investing. I named the books Investing 101 and Investing 201 because I wanted to give you a very simple, actionable, easy to understand and easy to follow blueprint to investing on your own and making money.

I believe you are safer if you control your own money, and I believe that you can do at least as well as most of the experts out there, but without all the fees they would charge.

RIDING THE CYCLES

2015 was a rough year for investing. It was the first year since 2008 that the entire market was down. Warren Buffett was down. The DOW, the NASDAQ and the S&P 500- they were all down.

This is actually a good thing in a way. We seem to need these down cycles from time to time. They seem to fuel the up cycles. It is almost as if the market, and the people investing in the markets, need a break every now and then. After the break, the market, and the people investing in them, seem to be refreshed and ready for another run.

The graph clip below is of the S&P 500 since about 1992. Overall, the S&P has been in an uptrend, but this clippet shows a period of time that the market was going a bit more sideways (a sideways channel), with prices fluctuating back and forth between around 800 to almost 1600. Notice the cycles wtihin this channel. You can see when the American people are optimistic by the upward trends. And you can see when the American people become pessimistic, as evidenced by the downward trends.

Chart courtesy of StockCharts.com

The idea of cycles or tides of the market brings up a very important point. Those who do well in the markets tend to recognize, understand and embrace these regular and unending market cycles. The cycles are not always as obvious in the above S&P 500 graph. Sometimes you see the cycles in an uptrending fund as a growth, a drawdown, followed by another growth to a higher level. Those who understand the markets buy when the market is low and reap their rewards when the markets return to an upward swing. They know that these cycles are inevitable, and they learn how to ride and profit from them. They know how to make the cycles work for them.

The average person doesn't seem to understand these cycles. They want the markets to go up smoothly and forever, and they try to ignore the fact that the up cycles always end, and that there will be a down cycle at some point. Unlike the rich, who buy when things are low and sell when they are high, the average person only buys during upswings in the markets, when things have been going up for a while, when it seems that the market just can't keep from going up. They buy when the market is reaching it's upward peak, but this is the point when the market tends to get exhausted, and soon has to drop. Notice in the last graph that this happens over and over. It is to be expetcted.

The smart money is buying more when the markets have dropped and the weak money is getting out, sitting on the sidelines, waiting for the next upward frenzy to attract them. It is well know that the rich buy "when there is blood on the streets". This is how they time the markets and make their fortunes. Following is yet another charting of the emotional reactions of the average person to market cycles. Every instance where the chart says "sell" is where the rich buy.

Understanding these cycles teaches you a very important lesson... most wealth is made in these cycles. Famous investors like Buffett and Schwabb have made their money because of these cycles. They learned how to ride them and how to use them to their advantage. We need to do the same. We need to ride the cycles, not swim against them. It is very hard to make money during the down cycles, and very easy to make money in the up cycles, if you know what you are doing.

There is no way to know how long any trend will last. You cannot predict, you can only intelligently react.

DON'T LISTEN TO THE NEWS, OR OTHER PEOPLE

Although you need to work on yourself so that you can make your decisions more logically and less emotionally, you still want to avoid, as much as possible, being exposed to things that affect you emotionally. No matter how good you get at controlling your emotions, too much exposure to emotion producing issues would affect just about anybody.

Here is a simple rule: don't watch the financial news and only tell like-minded and supportive people what you are doing. If you are in an investment and the "experts" on television tell you your investment is terrible, it will eat on you. No matter how sure of yourself you are, you will still have that doubt at the back of your mind. At least until you get good at this system.

The "experts" don't bother me at all now, but they used to. In fact, the experts are usually telling people to get into investments I have already made money on and am getting out of. Several people I have tried to help invest along the way tend to not get in when I tell them to. They wait until the television tells them to. Then, when I am close to getting out, the television is finally saying to get in. When I get out, they again wait on the television experts to agree. In the end, I usually make money doing it myself, and they typically lose money following the television- on the same exact investment.

The other part of the rule is to not tell anybody what you are doing, aside from like-minded individuals. One issue I have with human nature is that everybody knows everything there is to know about everything, even if they know nothing at all. If you tell somebody that you are controlling your own investments, they are going to start giving you all kinds of advice. Even if they have never invested a dime of their own money, they will still feel it their duty to tell you what they think about your project. Much of the time it will be out of sincere concern, but this is a mental stress you don't need to expose yourself to. It can affect your ability to make good decisions.

"Be careful", "That's dangerous", "I think you should do this", "I don't think you should do that", "So and so on TV says your investment is a dud", and so on. They mean well, I think, but the bottom line is that everybody wants to give you advice. And they will hound you and make you want to tear your hair out. Even when you can tell them that you are doing very, very well, it won't matter. Even if you are beating the S&P average of 10% per year by a landslide, consistently, every year, it won't matter.

Most people just cannot buck the system. The idea of doing their own thing and not following establishment's rules scare most people too much. The idea of you breaking the rules they live by also scares them to death for some reason. So be careful who you tell about your new venture. Even people that love you will drive you nuts. They are not trying to be mean, they honestly believe the TV over you. They are genuinely concerned for you. They don't and can't understand, and they think you are day trading or something crazy. They think this because the media teaches them this. You must do what the establishment says to do. 10% is all you can make. If you are bucking the system, you will lose. That is what the media has taught them, and they don't know any different.

Just avoid all this if you can. Trust me.

WHAT ABOUT OPTIONS?

Options are an investing strategy that is very different from the investing we are going over right now. It has to do with buying "options" to buy in the future. Only you never actually buy them, you only buy the "option" to, then trade those options as their value rises.

For right now, I belive you should just avoid options. I'm not a big fan of them. They are confusing. If you get bored with this system and want to branch out to options, have at it, but make sure you do your homework on them- take a few courses and paper trade them first before you jump in.

There are people I love and respect that are really into options, and that is great. For me- I have tried them and they are just not my thing. They seem to take more time to analyze and keep up with (I am used to just minutes per week), and they seem much less straightforward than what I am doing. If you want to trade options, TD Ameritrade requires much more information. They want to make sure you have enough experience and money to be playing with them. This says to me that options must be more risky for the average person than regular investing. I know some people claim they are simple and easy and very profitable- I just don't like them. I have used them, trained in them, and still lost money.

You may look into them and really enjoy them. I do not.

WHAT ABOUT IRAs, 401Ks AND THINGS LIKE THAT?

I am a bit wishy-washy on government-backed entities like IRAs and 401Ks. They seem to have big pluses, but they also have big minuses too. At least for me.

If you have one of these at work for your pension, no problem- use it. It can be part or all of your Conservative Retirement Fund. On the plus side, using one of these entities, your employer usually matches your contributions, up to a certain amount, which means free money. Also, you can delay paying taxes on the money you are investing until after retirement, when you are possibly in a lower income bracket. Since you are investing with pre-tax dollars, this also means you have more money in your account, gathering interest. And if your money is in one of these retirement vehicles, it is also protected automatically from predators, which is very good. Predators cannot go after retirement accounts.

The problems I have had personally with IRAs is that there are just too many confusing rules, regulations and penalties that seem to change yearly. There are also limits as to how much money you can put into an IRA each year, penalties for withdrawing even a penny, and strict rules on what you can and can't invest in (if you do it through your employer's plans). If you open your own, independent TD Ameritrate as an IRA you should be able to invest in whatever

WHAT ABOUT IRAS, 401KS AND THINGS LIKE THAT?

you want. You may not be able to invest in leveraged ETFs though. I'd ask to be sure.

What bothers me the most about these funds is that if you have an emergency and need to take out some of your own money, there are big penalties. This is a big deal for me. I have a friend that retired a little early, ran into an emergency and needed to get a little money out of his Roth IRA. He was told that the amount he needed was small enough that there would be no penalty fees. After he took the money out he was hit with a large penalty. He asked his financial advisor if he could turn around and put the money back in as if he hadn't taken it out and get his penalty fee waved. He was told yes, if he returned the money right away the fees would be waived. He put his money back in immediately, but not only did he not get the penalty fee back, the advisor that did it for him also got another cut of his money for putting it back into the account. Nobody, not even the financial experts in the know, seem to comprehend exactly how these plans work, that's how complicated and ever-changing they are.

If you do end up making enough money to retire early, before the age of 67, and if your money is in a Roth IRA, you won't be able to touch it yet. That is another thing to consider. Or if you do start drawing from it, there will be large penalties.

Bottom line is that I'm just not totally sure what to tell you about these entities. A financial advisor will absolutely be in favor of them, as it is a benefit to them. And they can be very convincing. I really like the tax deferral, which gives you more money to make interest on, and can make a really big difference. I also like the protection from predators. I don't like the confusing and ever changing nature of these programs though, and I don't like that there are limits as to how much you can put in, and penalties if you take any out early.

I'll leave it up to you to decide what you prefer. Just know that there are pluses and minuses with either choice. Having one through your employer is a definite yes in my opinion. It can be part or all of your Conservative Retirement Fund. But opening your early, Aggressive Retirement Fund with TD Ameritrade as a Roth IRA is just very iffy for me.

If you do not open your Early Retirement Fund as a Roth IRA, remember to open it as a trust, or some other entity that will protect your nest egg from predators. More on that now...

PROTECTING YOUR GOLDEN EGG!

When you start building up a nice little nest egg, it's a really good idea to protect it. In this day and age, people love to sue for every little thing. If you are ever in a car wreck, or somebody slips and falls and gets hurts on your property, or something similar occurs, you want to make sure nobody can come after the nest egg you've worked so hard to build.

To do that, first obtain good insurance coverage on everything you have- your house, your car, everything. If you have good insurance and something bad happens you should be covered. If you have bare bones insurance and get sued, the other party may come after you for more than your policy will pay. And if the other party's lawyer finds out you have a nest egg, the lawyer and the other party may try to win the lottery off of you.

In addition to a good liability policy on your house and car, talk to your insurance agent about an umbrella policy to cover anything over what your regular policy will cover. Say your auto liability policy covers up to $1 million. If you are in an accident where someone dies, and you get sued for lets say $2 million, an umbrella policy will cover anything over the amount your regular policy is limited to.

The second thing you need to do to protect your money is to talk with an attorney or an accountant about setting up a trust to put your nest egg in so that others can't get to it. This is what the rich do. They put the bulk of their wealth into some kind of a trust so that most of their assets are not in their names. Instead, the bulk of their assets are in the name of their trust. A trust is basically considered a business that you are running. You might be the President, your spouse the Vice President and Secretary, etc. So if a person with most of their money in a Trust gets sued, the person suing can only go after things that are in the name of the person they are suing. Since the trust is considered a business entity, and not an individual ownership, its assets are off limits to predators.

When you need money to live on, you simply take a "draw" of however much you need at the time, and leave the rest in. It is basically just a slightly more complicated banking account that you store all your stuff in until you need it.

You don't want to put everything you own into the trust though. For example, if your car is owned by the trust and you get into an auto accident, the other person can sue the owner of the car, which is the trust. So instead, you want to own your house and car, etc, but keep your wealth protected separately in a trust.

Family Limited Partnerships (FLPs) are a good choice these days for the average person to protect their money in this way. Or at least they were a few years ago. An FLP is basically a business partnership type of trust fund. It is technically a business that you and your spouse manage together. You and your partner do not own the money in the FLP, the FLP does, but you and your partner manage it. Whenever you need money, you and your partner take out "partnership draws". By doing this, it places your nest egg out of reach if someone tries to sue you, yet you still have full access to it.

There are a few rules to follow with all Trusts to make them protect you like they should. Make sure you ask your lawyer or accountant what the rules are and follow them to a T. The rules are not many and they are not hard, but if you violate them, the Trust won't protect your money, as it should.

Once you have an FLP, you can tell TD Ameritrade and they will transfer the name of the account from your name to the name of your Family Limited Partnership, thus putting your TD Ameritrade account out of reach of predators.

Again, if you have your money in an IRA, either through work or because you opened up your personal investing account in TD Ameritrade (or whichever brokerage you chose) as an IRA, then any money in that account is automatically protected. Retirement money is off limits to predators.

KEEPING UP WITH YOUR PROGRESS

For those of you that are like me and really like to keep up with everything, you are going to want to keep up with your returns to see what percent you are making with your money. Personally, every year, I keep up with the percent return I made and I compare it to the percent return of the S&P 500, which is the main benchmark of the market. If I feel like it, I may compare it to the DOW and Nasdaq too.

For a simple method of keeping track of your returns, simply write down how much money you have in your TD Ameritrade account on January 1st of the current year. Then on December 31st write down how much you have now. The difference is your total fund growth for the year.

Here is an example:

Balance on January 1st	$10,000
Balance on December 31st	$12,000
= Total Investment Fund Growth	= $2,000

Now to get your percent growth for the year:

Total Growth / Starting Balance	$2,000/$10,000 = .2
	.2 x 100 = 20%

So that gives you your total growth for the year of $2,000, which comes to 20%. The only problem is that includes the amount of money you put into your Retirement and Early Retirement Funds over the course of the year. To correct for that:

Balance on January 1st:	$10,000
Balance on December 1st	$12,000
- Amount you added to the fund that year	- $500
= Investment Growth for the Year	= $1,500

Now to get your percent growth for the year of your investments alone:

Investment Growth / Starting Balance	$1,500 / $10,000 = .15
	.15 x 100 = 15%

Now you know how much your overall investment fund grew this year, including the money you added to the fund during the year: $2,000, which is 20%.

You now also know how much your investments grew on their own: $1,500, which is 15%.

Look up how much the Dow, S&P and Nasdaq made that year and compare your 15% to it to see how well you are investing.

It is important, at least for me, to know both the total growth of my portfolio for the year (including money I added to the fund) as well as how much the account grew without the added money. Knowing how well the fund did without counting the money I added tells me how well my investing strategy is working, while knowing the total growth lets me know how much closer I am getting to my overall money goal. And in that regard, the money I add to the account each year also counts.

A DREAM COME TRUE- LIVING OFF YOUR INVESTMENTS

We are on the last step. When you save up enough money to live off of your investments, let's say one million dollars, you need to know how much you can spend each year. You don't want to take more out of your investments than you are making in returns. The goal is to leave the original amount alone, lets say $1 million, and live only off the interest it is making for you. You want to live off your money generator, without hurting the generator itself; pluck leaves from your money tree, but leave the trunk and branches unscathed to grow more.

Let's say you have a million invested, and that it made you 10% last year:

Original Nest Egg Amount	1 million dollars
Interest Earned Last Year	10%, which is $100,000

You can spend UP TO however much interest you made last year. So in the above example, you CAN live off of UP TO $100,000 this year. No more. BUT, it is smarter to live off less. Many experts recommend living off 4% of however much you have, total. If you have saved up $1 million, that means you can take out $40,000 per year.

By not spending every bit of the interest we make each year, it allows the nest egg to keep growing a bit, even in retirement. But also, if you average 10% per year (we are hoping to do better than that, but let's use that as an example), then you are not making 10% *every* year; you are making that on AVERAGE. One year you might make 20% and the next 0%. If you spend ALL the interest during the good years, you might not have any at all during the bad.

Remember though, if you have a pension, social security, etc, those sources will be making you money too.

No matter how you decide to do it, never take out more than the interest from the year before. That would be like having a money tree making you $100,000 in leaves per year, but you get greedy and cut the tree down. You can either live off the leaves forever, or kill the tree and have a limited amount of money. Forever is smarter.

Once you decide how much money you are going to live on this year, do not take out all the money you need at once. Only take out what you need as you need it. If your portfolio has $1 million in it, and you are going to take out $40,000 to live on this year, then that comes to a little more than $3,333 per month. Once per month, simply take out the $3,333 for that month.

If you took the full amount at once for the whole year, then you would be removing that money from the safety of your trust for one thing. If you got sued, that amount wouldn't be safe. Also, money left in could still be earning interest until you needed it. By only taking out what you need, when you need it, you are leaving whatever you can in to make you even more money until you need it. Even in retirement, you can let your nest egg grow so that you

A DREAM COME TRUE- LIVING OFF YOUR INVESTMENTS

can end up making even more interest, which means you have more money you can take home.

If you have $1 million, and made 10%, or $100,000 last year, but only are taking out $40,000 this year, then you are leaving in $60,000 in interest and you now have $1,060,000. And if that goes up 10% this year, then it will be at $1,166,000 by the end of the year. The next year, taking 4% out will give you $46,640 for the year. So your payments go up each year, helping with inflation.

Two more things: First, you will be paying taxes on the money you remove from your investments. When you are ready to start living off your investments, sit down with your accountant or tax professional and have them help you estimate how much you need to put aside for taxes. You don't want to get in trouble with the IRS, or end up having to take a chunk out of your Money Generator to pay Uncle Sam for back-taxes.

Secondly, if this method of taking money out sounds too complicated, talk to a financial advisor about annuities or some other simple method of storing your nest egg. Say your goal is one million dollars. Once you have that nest egg, you could put the nest egg into an anuity or something similar. After you put your lump sum in, an annuity will pay you a certain amount for the rest of your life. This simplifies things greatly. You now just sit back and let them send you checks for the rest of your life.

A lot of people like annuities. A lot of people don't. There are high up front fees, but at the same time they are very convenient. If you are interested just talk to a financial advisor or accountant and see what you think.

I tend to avoid having someone manage my money when I'm trying to build wealth, but once it is built, I am in favor of storing it in something safe like an annuity. I would not, however, take my nest egg and let a financial advisor put that money back into the market. I have seen too many financial advisors lose people's nest eggs. Safe annuities? Yes. Let them invest your money? No.

SIMPLIFIED SUMMARY AND ACTION STEPS

1. Figure out how much money you will need, at a bare minimum, to retire on comfortably by the age of 67.
2. Your pension through your employer, if you have one, may cover some or all of this amount.
3. Any amount above what your pension will provide needs to be put aside as a bill that is paid to your Retirement Fund, which is opened up in TD Ameritrade, or your brokerage of choice.
4. You may want to set your account up with TD Ameritrade as some sort of trust, to protect it as it grows. Setting it up as a Roth IRA is another possibility that will protect it.
5. Invest your retirement money into SPY, an S&P 500 index fund. This is your Retirement Fund, invested conservatively.
6. Start keeping up with your bills so that you know how much money you spend on necessities versus your income. The leftover money is Excess Money that is going to be split between Early Retirement Investments and having Fun Money.
7. It is best, but not mandatory, to use Early Retirement Money initially to pay off debt and build a savings account before starting to invest it in your Early Retirement Fund.
8. During this time, start paper-trading so that by the time you are ready to invest, you have paper-traded for a while and may be ready to use real money.

9. Once the debts are paid and you have a good savings account, start investing your Early Retirement Fund Money.
10. Protect your money as it starts to grow with good insurance. You also should have, as mentioned in step 4, set up your account as a trust or in some other way that protects your money from predators.
11. Keep up with how fast your money is growing and compare it to the the S&P 500, and maybe the DOW and Nasdaq to make sure you are doing as well as you should.
12. When you can live off the interest on your investments, do.
13. If you keep working, simply invest all the money you make from working in your investments.
14. Now you are earning your money once and spending it forever!!
15. You will never earn and then spend another dollar. You may earn more money, but you will never spend it. You will only spend its children.

YOU VS YOU, BEFORE AND AFTER

Now that you have made it to the end of this book, I want you to ask yourself a very simple, but very serious question: Who is better at investing- the you that existed before reading this book, or the you that has finished the book?

Unless something has gone seriously wrong, the "after" you should be able to beat the absolute socks off of the "before" you at investing.

Think of how much better you will be with experience. Just keep it simple and take baby steps, with your goal always to be just a little better than you were before.

SHAMELESSLY PUSHING MY NEWSLETTER SERVICE

If you think you are better at investing and money management now than you were before reading this book, think of how much more quickly you can improve if you have someone there holding your hand, telling you what to do for a while.

I have repeatedly, shamelessly pushed my newsletter throughout this book, and I am going to continue to do so. I truly wish I had someone in the beginning that could have realistically helped me along. Not a salesman pushing all the newest, greatest stocks, promising the moon and stars, but a realistic investor that had been there and done that, and knew what to do. I lost so much money learning how to invest.

I have friends that live close to me that follow my method, and I can tell you without hesitation that, at least in the beginning, you will need help. Investing is so emotional and counterintuitive that we all need support. It can also be so frustrating and boring and slow that most people just can't seem to do it. Most people have a hard time hanging in there during anything but upward runs. My friends and I, I have found, must talk regularly, especially when the market is declining, or in a sideways channel. When the market is climbing, they seem to need no help at all- they seem to know it all then. ☺

SHAMELESSLY PUSHING MY NEWSLETTER SERVICE

When I was starting, I followed so many gurus and newsletters that were just hype. With them, every newsletter annnounced a new greatest investment opportunity ever. I understand- they do this to keep subscriber's interest. But it is impossible to get into everything they recommend, as every single month it is going to be something new and different. And, their newsletter is just a hook really. They get you excited about the possibility of being rich, and then use that to sell you more and more of their products. I have no more products, just my books and my newsletter.

I am not in any way saying that I am the greatest investor ever, and I am not promising you anything but my experience. I do not know if you will get rich on my advice, I only know what has worked for me so far and am willing to share it with you. Compared to the big newsletters out there, my newsletter is absolutely boring, so be warned. It is only a few times a year that I recommend action. But it is based on a mature, reliable system of managing and investing money, not on hype, keeping you hooked and trying to sell you more.

At $10 a month, $2.5 a week, it is a steal. I truly believe that. I truly believe you need it, if you are at all like the average beginner at investing, And if you don't make that money back, many times over in your investing, something has really, really gone wrong.

I shamelessly plug my newseltter because I absolutely believe in it. The newsletter is sent out once a week on Monday mornings. Here is a link to signup:
https://www.matthewbarnes-101.com/the-money-club-newsletter

FURTHER RESOURCES

I know this information can be a little overwhelming if you are a beginner, even a simplified version like my system. I have been reading books on money management and wealth building since I entered the workplace years ago- I knew early on that I wanted to be free of the tyranny of money. Along the way there were several books and systems of managing money and ways of investing that resonated with me and helped shape the system I now use. I'd like to recommend a few to you.

The first is *Rich Dad, Poor Dad* by Robert Kiyosaki. This book goes very deeply into the idea of using the money you earn to buy a money generator instead of spending it all. I highly recommend this book for a deeper understanding of this concept.

The second is *Financial Peace* by Dave Ramsey. Many of you have probably heard of this book. Ramsey introduced me to the idea of compartmentalizing money. I don't do it quite the same way as he taught, but my system of money management was influenced greatly by his.

If It Doesn't Go Up Don't Buy It by Al Thomas, *How to Make the Stock Market Make Money for You* by Ted Warren, the works of Ken Roberts, *How I made $2,000,000 in the Stock Market* by Nicolas Darvas, and the works of Burton H. Pugh are the books that most influenced the system I use now for investing. I do not quite do what they taught, but their unique ways of looking at investing got me to where my investing is today. Each of these teachers developed a unique, non-mainstream approach to investing, and as a result, made a lot more money than the "experts" that followed establishment rules. I very much appreciate these innovators' ability to break from the norm and pioneer a new way. I am now coming to realize just how much gumption it takes to do such a thing.

BIO

Matt is an avid, maybe obsessive learner. He was born in Greenville, NC and has lived in New Bern, Roanoke Rapids, Henderson (where he spent most of his childhood) and Raleigh, where he attended North Carolina State University.

For more information on Matt or his works, his current website is www.MatthewBarnes-101.com, or http://www.amazon.com/Matthew-S.-Barnes/e/B00SDYKSZ2

> "I am still learning."
> - Michelangelo

LETTER FROM THE AUTHOR

Dear Reader,

Thank you for reading! You've made my day ☺

I hope you enjoyed *Investing 201*. More than that- I hope that I have helped you to make your life better.

If you liked this book, please leave me a positive review on Amazon.

The number of reviews and the number of stars awarded in those reviews can literally make or break a book's success these days. Your review can be just one or two words- it doesn't have to be a detailed summary, or anything close. Anything would be greatly appreciated.

The big publishers know how important reviews are, and therefore pay for lots and lots of them. Independent writers like me don't have those kind of resources, so we rely on you good people.

Thank you for spending time with me!

Matthew Barnes

www.ingramcontent.com/pod-product-compliance
Lightning Source LLC
Chambersburg PA
CBHW030702220526
45463CB00005B/1863